LIFE
IN THE
SLOW
LANE

Also by S. D. Gaede:

Belonging: Our Need for Community in Church and Family

For All Who Have Been Forsaken

Where Gods May Dwell: Understanding the Human Condition

LIFE
IN THE
SLOW
LANE

The Benefits of Not Getting What
You Want When You Want It

S.D. GAEDE

ZondervanPublishingHouse
Grand Rapids, Michigan

A Division of HarperCollins*Publishers*

Life in the Slow Lane
Copyright © 1991 by S. D. Gaede

Requests for information should be addressed to:
Zondervan Publishing House
1415 Lake Drive, S.E.
Grand Rapids, Michigan 49506

Library of Congress Cataloging-in-Publication Data

Gaede, S. D.
    Life in the slow lane : the benefits of not getting what you want
when you want it / Stan Gaede.
        p.   cm.
    ISBN 0-310-53201-9
    1. Christian life—1960– 2. Simplicity—Religious aspects—
Christianity. 3. Gaede, S. D. I. Title.
BV4501.2.G273   1991
248.4—dc20   90–46374
                                                                    CIP

Designed by Louise Bauer

Printed in the United States of America

91 92 93 94 95 96 / AK / 10 9 8 7 6 5 4 3 2 1

To Heather with love,
For graciously enduring the slow lane

Contents

Preface

Growing up, I always envisioned myself driving in the fast lane. Sitting squarely between Mom and Dad in the front seat of our '55 Chrysler, I'd press my head as close to the windshield as possible, fix my eyes on the traffic ahead, and try to forget the facts around me—especially that I was sitting between Mom and Dad in a '55 Chrysler! The dream, of course, was that I was in another body (older), another automobile (sportier), and in another lane (faster).

The details of the dream changed with the times. When I was eleven, I saw myself in a '57 T-bird, with a large collie at my side, cruising down Central Avenue and waving to my friends. By the time I was sixteen, the T-bird had been replaced by a Porsche, the collie by a blonde, and the closest thing my friends got to a wave was the curl of smoke from my tail pipes. Needless to say, Central Avenue wasn't in the picture anymore either, having been superseded by a freeway, a drag strip, or Laguna Canyon Road, depending upon the requirements of the fantasy.

At various points in my life, the dream nearly came

true. While I never managed to own the car of my dreams, my best friend did, and I gained a good deal of vicarious satisfaction driving around with him on weekends. A few years later, the Lord sufficiently clouded a beautiful young woman's judgment to enable her to fall in love with me, and I did in fact marry the woman of my dreams. And though I haven't become wealthy, I've been in a position to mingle with the rich periodically and sample certain delicacies from their cuisine. The point is, I have been able to make a few forays into the fast lane. And, if truth be known, I still have visions of driving there permanently someday.

Nevertheless, I spend most of my time in the slow lane. And I have to admit that as much as I don't want to be there, the slow lane has certain advantages. Some days I don't want to move quickly, for one thing. I just don't have the energy for it; or I don't want to miss the scenery along the way. I also like the people I meet in the slow lane. On the whole they are a lot nicer than those in the fast lane. More accommodating. Less pretentious. And a whole lot easier to talk to.

Most importantly (and I almost cringe to say this), the slow lane has been a great learning experience for me. It has forced me to come to terms with life—and the meaning of God's truth in the midst of that life—in a way that the fast lane never has. Nor, I suspect, ever could.

Don't get me wrong. The slow lane is no piece of cake. I am forever frustrated with cars in front of me that seem content to move at a snail's pace, and trucks that smell like the south end of a northbound mule—and are, for some strange reason, impassable. And I'm not too fond of being blown off the road by Porsches and Lamborghinis, either, as they race around me at breakneck speed and look so very good doing it.

But the object of driving is not just looking good on the road, nor having a great time along the way. The object is making it home, and getting there in a way that pleases the Father who waits for us at the end of our journey. That's what *Life in the Slow Lane* is all about. Making it home—and learning from the journey what I need to know to prepare myself to meet the Father once I get there.

1

LIFE AS A
CHILD

Things

I grew up in a rural portion of the San Joaquin Valley, about a hundred miles north of Los Angeles. I don't know what images that conjures up in your mind, but whatever they are, they're wrong, though the fault is not your own. The Valley is a hard place to describe. Every adjective seems to lead one astray.

For example, while the San Joaquin is in California, it is not a land of Jacuzzies, yachts, or wine-and-cheese parties. The Valley is essentially a desert-cum-garden, and the people there are a fairly rugged lot by California standards: their tan is more leathery, their taste is less refined (Coors and pit barbecue, not quiche with chablis), and their lingo has a distinct twang to it. In fact, in terms of lifestyle you'd be better off thinking of the Midwest than California, since that's where many of its residents came from in the first place.

But in other ways the Midwest won't do as a descriptor, either, because the Sooners and Jawhawks who started farming this region during the early part of the century have been greatly changed by their California experience. Their farms are not homey little places with

13

hogs and silos and two-story homesteads. They are businesses first and foremost, some of the most productive in the world, and they have been designed for efficiency, not for Norman Rockwell. To a midwesterner, the Valley looks fast paced, calculating, and mechanical, without the charm or tradition of the Plains. To a Joaquinian, the Midwest looks dull as dishwater. So there is, today, a vast difference between the two.

Like the rest of California, the Valley has been shaped by the mix of people that occupy it. The midwesterners have been joined by southerners, Hispanics, immigrants, and business-types, and each have left their mark. Radios play country music as well as rock. Conversations occur in Spanish as well as Valley twang. And farmers have names like Lachenmaier, Torrigiani, and Wong, as well as Smith, Lane, and Williams.

And of course Gaede. Which gets us to the point of this discussion. My father too was a San Joaquin farmer, which means he probably doesn't fit your stereotype of the average American farmer. In fact, he moved into farming from the grocery business, not because he had a deep love of the land, not because he wanted to feed the nation, not because he loved to get up early in the morning and watch the plants reach for the sky, not for any reason at all except to make a living. For him it was a business, pure and simple, and it was the business end of the operation that occupied most of his time and thinking.

Some people say farmers are romantics and dreamers, and that's what sustains them through years of depression and heartache. That may be the case, but it bears no relation to my father. If he ever had a romantic thought about farming, it was the best-kept secret west of the Pecos. I remember driving by our farm one morning and commenting on the deep green beauty of the young potato plants; he looked absolutely stunned by the idea and probably spent the rest of the day trying to figure out how I had arrived at such a conclusion. If he hadn't prospered at farming, he would have happily sold the farm and done something more profitable. Where the farm was concerned, he didn't have a sentimental bone in his body.

None of this should be construed to suggest that my father was a crass businessman without feelings or emotions. He was nothing of the sort. *Things* were to be manipulated, but *people* were not. And for people, a tear would come to his eye at the drop of a hat. Even at age fifty-five, if you even mentioned the name of his favorite grade-school teacher, his eyes grew misty. If you talked about other people behind their backs—even your enemies—he would rebuke you immediately. And if another farmer was in financial difficulty and was selling his farm as a result, my dad's heart would ache for him. But if it was Dad's farm that needed peddling? Sell the thing and get on with life.

This approach to *things* made him a bit frustrating to deal with at times—and a very effective businessman. One of my most vivid memories is of my dad purchasing a new car. We would walk into the showroom together, and I—having researched the matter in detail—would tell Dad precisely the kind of car we should buy, including color, style, and a hundred other things. Dad would listen, ask a few embarrassing questions ("Why do we need the larger engine when the small one costs less, gets better gas mileage, and has a good track record?"), and then finally turn his attention to the salesman, who was more than likely following us all over the showroom during this time, unsuccessfully trying to get my dad's attention.

The salesman would proceed to take us over to his desk and ask us one of those "salesy" questions, like, "Well, now, what kind of car are you interested in?" I would bite every time and immediately launch into a description of my dream car. The salesman would smile and surely think to himself, *Gotcha!*

My dad, however, wouldn't say a word. He would just sit there, politely nod his head once or twice, and let the salesman ramble. Which, of course, the fellow would do. At first, the salesman would think that he was really making progress, since my dad was listening and he was controlling the conversation. But eventually it would dawn on him that he wasn't receiving any feedback whatsoever. And that's when he would start getting more than a tad anxious. Things would become especially tense, however, when we got down to price.

"Well, Mr. Gaede, how would you like to drive that car home this afternoon?"

No response.

"Well, I'll tell you what I'm going to do. This is a brand new 1961 model and the sticker price is $3,200. But I'm going to let you have it for $2,995. What do you say?"

"Great!" I would say under my breath, smiling so broadly my cheeks would practically split from the strain. But then I would peek over at my father and he would be just sitting there, his face expressionless, and his eyes darting around the room, glancing at the car once or twice, down to his twitching thumb for just a moment, and finally coming to rest on the ceiling above. His lips wouldn't even part.

"Well, Mr. Gaede, it may be possible to shave just a little more off that price," the salesman continued, trying to do something to compensate for all the silence. "Tell you what I'm going to do. I'll talk to my boss and see if I can get it for you for a flat $2,900. Would you be willing to take it for that?"

Again, no response.

A powerful silence ensued, the salesman playing

with his pencil and my dad uttering not a sound. Salesmen, I have learned, can stand about 2.2 seconds of such serenity, after which they begin to draw Mickey Mouse ears on their legal pad, roll around on their seat, answer other people's telephones, tell you about their pet greyhound, and generally question the meaning of life. If it were a normal conversation, the silence wouldn't be a problem: One would simply tell Mr. Gaede to wake up or else bid him a fond farewell. But this is not a normal conversation. The salesman thinks he is on the verge of selling a car. That means he can't break off the relationship, nor can he be rude. Rather, he must somehow keep the conversation going, even though Mr. Gaede isn't going anywhere with the conversation. So about this time, the poor fellow would excuse himself, pretend that he had to talk the deal over with his boss, but would probably head straight for the bathroom.

"Dad, that's a great deal," I would chime in the minute he was gone. "Aren't you interested?"

My father would smile. "It is a nice car, isn't it? What do you suppose your mom would think of it?"

"Oh, she'd love it," I would say, after which I would carry on another extended monologue about all the advantages of the vehicle and how well it would fit into our garage, not to mention our lives. Dad would listen attentively and smile—only because he knew I was excited about the car—but he wouldn't commit himself in the least. Finally, the salesman would return.

"Well, now, tell you what I'm going to do. I've just been talking to Mr. Bimbo himself, and he said we really need to move that car. He's willing to let you have it for—rock bottom, now—$2,850!"

Unbelievable, I thought to myself! *They're practically giving the car away. Even Dad won't be able to resist that offer.*

"Uh ... I was wondering," Dad would finally say, "does the car have air-conditioning?"

"Well, no ... no it doesn't, Mr. Gaede. But," picking up steam here, "we can sure install that for you. Let me see here. Yes. We can add air-conditioning for $399. Would you like that, Mr. Gaede?"

"Hummm.... That's getting a little high, I'm afraid...." And then Dad would look back at the car and lapse back into his silent mode.

"Look, let me see what I can do for you, Mr. Gaede," and off the salesman would go for another therapy session with Mr. Bimbo. In no time, he was back with the good news.

"Mr. Gaede, you caught Mr. Bimbo in a great mood today. He's willing to let you have the air-conditioner for only $150. That means you can have the car, with the air-conditioner, for $3,000 ... and, Mr. Gaede," he looked at Dad with the eyes of a bloodhound, "that's really as low as I can go."

"Okay, then. Thank you for your time, Mr. Salesman," Dad would say cordially, stretching out his hand in front of him, and pulling himself out of his chair. "My son tells me this is a nice car you've got here. And I really appreciate your showing it to us." And then an astonished salesman would watch as Mr. Gaede and son would walk out of the showroom.

Now, there are two things that need to be kept in mind about this whole episode. One, my dad's behavior was not simply a ploy or a ruse to manipulate the salesman into giving him a better deal. And second, the whole scene—which I had the opportunity to observe on innumerable occasions—used to drive me absolutely bananas. Since the second point is the more obvious of the two, let me begin with the first.

Most readers no doubt assume, and I'm confident the salesman believed, that my dad's behavior was designed to unnerve the salesman and thereby produce a lower-cost vehicle. Nothing could be further from the truth. Certainly, my dad was looking for the best price possible, but he was totally incapable of such an artful manipulation of social conditions to achieve that end. The basis for Dad's behavior was not economics but worldview. He simply had no need whatsoever to buy the car.

As a result, when he walked out of the showroom, the car and all its putative advantages would simply vanish from his mind, and he would be off and running, doing other things. Sometimes the salesman would contact him a day or two later and offer him a better deal. And sometimes the offer would interest Dad enough that he would reconsider the matter and possibly even purchase the car. But not necessarily. The bottom line for Dad was always, Is the purchase necessary and is it a good use of our money? No deal could dissuade him if the answer to those questions was "no."

The consequence of this approach was that, even though Dad was a modestly successful farmer, some of our things—including cars—were pretty ripe before we got rid of them. Not all things, mind you, but some things. Dad lived with a tractor longer than any farmer I ever knew—sometimes far too long, according to those of us who had to sit on them all day long. He simply saw no reason to spend huge sums of money on a new tractor when the old one still ran or could be fixed. He didn't farm for show. On the other hand, when a new piece of equipment would pay for itself—like a potato harvester, for example—he was willing to invest staggering amounts of money in state-of-the-art machinery. The bottom line, again, was stewardship, not self-aggrandizement.

And that's what used to drive me up the wall. Because I was not detached from things. I liked things. I liked the way they looked. I liked the way they felt. I liked the way they moved. I especially liked the way they moved me. And cars moved me in more ways than one. Thus, the fact that we were still plugging along in our old '55 Chrysler in 1961 was an embarrassment. And the fact that Dad was turning his back on a great deal and a great car was maddening. And disappointing. And in moments of deep aesthetic rapture, even fundamentally wrong.

Indeed, sitting there in the showroom, watching the salesman squirm and listening to my dad's silence, I could become downright moral about the whole thing. What right did my dad have putting the salesman through this ordeal, anyway? Or me, for that matter? The salesman was just trying to make a living, for goodness sake. Why put the man in Bellevue for the sake of a few hundred dollars? And me? I was just trying to look out for the welfare of the family. Was it safe to let Mom drive around in a car with 120,000 miles on it? Was it even right? Didn't she deserve something with a little more class? Shouldn't Dad be driving a car more befitting of his station in life? Wouldn't I look good sitting in the passenger seat and—in a few years—behind the steering wheel? Wasn't a purchase really the right thing to do? The good, prudent, proper, wonderful thing to do?

What escaped my attention at the time, and eludes me even still, is that the salesman's strain—and mine— was not induced by my father but by a clash of two different worldviews. We cared about the car; my father did not. We had a personal interest in seeing a transaction take place; my father was profoundly disinterested. We thought the car would improve our place in life; my father thought it would get us from one place to another, just like our '55 Chrysler. Two different perspectives on a car. Two different angles on life.

I don't think my dad's view of things was a hundred percent correct, by the way. Even today. The salesman had a right to feed his family, after all. And I sometimes thought my dad failed to fully appreciate things. When the interstate bypass first circumvented Albuquerque, I tried to talk Dad into driving through the middle of town anyway, just so we could see the heart of the city; when he rejected my proposal, I accused him of not having any romance in his soul. That brought a laugh from my mother and a wince from my dad, but it didn't do a thing to the direction of the car. Nevertheless, I still prefer Albuquerque to the interstate. And I think he should have as well.

But on the whole, Dad had it just about right with things. What is clear to me, at the very least, is that I was quite wrong about the car. Automobiles are convenient forms of transportation, and their form and function sometimes deserve genuine admiration. But as sources of prestige and self-respect, they are surely deficient. The '55 Chrysler made that abundantly clear. At birth, it seemed like the cat's pajamas, an entrée into the world of high times and high living. By 1961, it looked like an anemic hippo with fins—Big Bird just before he cashes in the chips.

Why is it that we invest so much personal significance in things anyway? Especially when we know that tomorrow they'll be old or tarnished or stolen? It isn't simply that we think too highly of things. We think too lowly of ourselves. We don't have enough self-respect to keep things in proper perspective. My father had the good sense to realize that his worth was not dependent on the things over which he had been given dominion, but on the One who had given him dominion in the first place.

I just wish good sense were an inherited trait.

People

My dad had it just about right with people as well.

I remember the family driving home from church one Sunday night and seeing a man in a trench coat, walking on the wrong side of the road, weaving on and off the pavement. My dad slowed down as we approached the figure and, while everyone in the car gawked, Dad tried to keep as much distance as possible between the man and our Chrysler. He did that for the man's safety, of course, not the Chrysler's. But I remember thinking—as we were going by and I tried to catch a glimpse of the shadowy figure's face—that the distance was comforting to me as well.

When we finally arrived home, Dad stopped the car just short of the garage and allowed everyone to jump out. I thought that was odd since we usually went right into the garage. But Dad had his own reasons, and he didn't always feel compelled to share them with me. And at that point, I didn't feel particularly compelled to discover what they were. The trench-coat figure had sent a chill down my spine, and I was anxious to get into the house and warm up. Besides, *Bonanza* was already half over.

I sat in the middle of the front seat, however, with Mom to my right, so my quick exit had to wait. (Even for a ten-year-old, crawling over your mother right after a church service for *Bonanza's* sake didn't seem quite right.) I sat there patiently, waiting for Mom to collect her purse, loose bulletins, hairpins, a Bible, church memorabilia, the Dead Sea Scrolls, etc. Finally, the big moment came. Mom slipped out the door. And I, having timed my escape with precision, was less than a hairsbreadth behind her. Just as my right foot hit the pavement, though, I felt a hand on my shoulder.

"Stan," came my father's voice, "I want you to stay in the car with me. I'm going to go back to see if that man needs help."

I quickly looked around the car to see if he had another son named Stan.

"Uh . . . you mean me, Dad?" I finally said, still desperately hoping for some alternative explanation.

"Yup," he quipped as he put the car back in gear. "Close the door."

"Uh . . . Dad," I said, leaving the door ajar and my foot firmly planted on the driveway, "You know, I . . . I'm really tired. And I've got a lot of homework to do. And my room needs cleaning. And that guy was probably just a jogger anyway, don't you think? It's a new fad—trench-coat jogging in the middle of the night. It really helps to build up your shoulder muscles and does wonders for night vision. They say that it . . ."

Dad looked at me without enthusiasm. And I slowly slipped back into the car and closed my mouth. It was one of the lower points in my prepubescent career, presenting me with a classic Catch-22. If I had put my foot down and said, "Dad, I don't want to go," he would have said, "Fine," driven away without comment, and I would have felt like squat. On the other hand, if I went with my father, I had every reason to believe that I was going to die.

I chose death, in large part, because it seemed like the easier thing to do. So we proceeded to back out of the driveway and headed down the road. As the engine picked up speed, I suddenly felt compelled to "pray without ceasing": "Lord, make him disappear, make him disappear, make him disappear. . . ."

A few minutes into the incantation, however, I started to question its value. The Lord did not have a habit of making people disappear, I knew, and I began to doubt he would even want to. I decided to change strategies and ask for something I knew that God would want.

Heal him, Lord! I cried out in my mind. Right there on the side of the road, heal him of his infirmities. Heal him of his iniquities. Take care of his insecurities too. Do it all, Lord. Right now. Before we even get there, Lord, do a miracle and rescue that man from his wicked ways. Heal him, Lord. Heal him, Lord. Heal him, Lord. . . .

The Chrysler and I were both in high gear when the man's figure appeared again on the side of the road, precisely at the spot we had last encountered him. *Rats,* I thought to myself, *I knew the disappearing prayer was a bad one. Maybe he's been healed,* I continued to hope. *Maybe he's been miraculously transformed!*

Not a chance. The figure was just as hunched over and pathetic looking as before. My prayers had not worked, not even the healer.

Things were rapidly going downhill when my father pulled the car to the side of the road, just a few yards from the rubbery figure. He put the transmission in "park" but left the engine running. As his hand reached for the door, he paused for just a moment, seemingly studying the figure who was now standing directly in front of us.

"Stan," he carefully said, "I want you to stay in the car."

"Riiiiight, Dad!" I responded with all the vigor of a West Point cadet. "Anything you say! Let me hold down the old fort for you, Dad. The car's in good hands. Don't worry about a thing."

As my father eased out of the car and walked over to the man, I tried to watch what he was doing but found it difficult from my vantage point under the dashboard of the car. He was talking with the fellow, I could tell that. But about what, I couldn't imagine. I pulled my head a little higher, only to discover that—"Oh no!"—Dad was bringing him over to the car! I tried to crawl farther under the dashboard, but got caught in the wires. Suddenly, the back door swung open and the terrifying creature lurched into the rear seat of our car. The door closed. And then ... we were ... alone.

As my dad walked around to the driver's side of the car, I tried to untangle myself from the wires. I was in deeper than I thought and, in due time, became more concerned about the wires than the stranger. I could just see the morning's headlines: *Son Strangled Under Dashboard While Father Tries To Be Good Samaritan; Family Apologizes*. It was not an auspicious departure.

Struggling to save face, now, I managed to climb back into the front seat before my father returned to the car. The move was the first constructive thing I'd done all evening and it gave me a bolt of courage. I began to think that I might be able to salvage my dignity after all. As Dad slipped into his seat, therefore, I screwed up my courage for the ultimate act of bravery.

"Hi," I said happily, as I popped up for a quick peek into the back seat of the car. "How's it going?"

It was a dumb question, to say the least, and under

normal circumstances I would have spent a substantial amount of energy simply contemplating how utterly banal and ridiculous it was. But something interrupted my thinking process. Something, or someone, that abruptly made my self-absorption seem pathetic and my worries ludicrous. The shadowy figure—the trench-coat stranger, the great and evil creature—was nothing more than a shivering, inebriated, and completely disoriented old woman. Nothing more. And nothing less.

As embarrassment replaced fear, I finally began to make a contribution to the evening, finding a blanket in the trunk, wrapping it around the old woman's legs, asking her how she felt, and generally acting as if she were a needy human being. It was a new approach for me. And as we took her home that evening and placed her in her bed, I couldn't help noticing that I had undergone a kind of liberation as a result. I had been freed from fear, for one thing. But also freed from myself. Freed, in other words, to give away some of what had been freely given to me. And for the first time in a long time, I felt good.

It was a freedom my dad had known all along, of course. For unlike his son, he had seen a human being from the start—not a caricature—and he responded in kind. Just as he did not make *things* more than things, he did not make *people* less than people. He didn't reduce them to drunks, or freaks, or enemies. Nor did he elevate them to saints. People were people. Worthy, because they were created in the image of God. Pitiful, because they did battle with sin and lost. To be served, because of Jesus—who served us—and who did battle with sin and won. No hairsplitting theology. No questions asked about who is my neighbor or who is not. Just a faithful picture of the human condition. And a faithful response.

To this day, it is not a response I find easy to emulate. Soon after we were married, Judy and I were

traveling down the interstate one morning in a rush to get
to church. As we streaked along the highway, we passed
a man who was on the side of the road trying to change a
flat tire.

"Did you see that, hon?" Judy asked us as we
whizzed by.

"Yup," I responded, sounding more like my father
every day.

"He didn't look like he was having an easy time of
it, Hon," she continued.

"Nope," I continued in style.

"Do you think we ought to go back and help?" she
finally asked, though she had been asking it all along.

"Judy, we're on the freeway," I finally said. "It will
take ten minutes to get off the highway, turn around, and
get back to the man. Besides, we're late for church—not
by my own doing, I might add—and I've got my best pair
of pants on. This is no time to play the Good Samaritan."

"Okay," she said, disapprovingly, as the sound of
my own words rang in my ears.

Late for church.

Best pair of pants.

No time to play the Good Samaritan.

It eventually dawned on me that, in my rush to
worship the One who taught us about the Good Samaritan, I was willing to play the priest and Levite. Of course,
it was not the time to be the Good Samaritan. It was time
to be religious instead. For that, I had plenty of time. But
being a Good Samaritan, that's another story. For that,
there is never enough time. Keepers of the clock do many
things well, but Samariting is not one of them. And in
our family, I am the keeper of the clock.

Under the weight of the Teacher and his Teaching,
not to mention the heavy sighs of my wife, I finally
pulled the car off the road, turned around, and made my
way back down the freeway. When we arrived, we found

a man who was too weak to pull his spare out of the trunk and too bright to figure out how to work the jack. In less than five minutes, I had the spare on, and the man off and running.

Five piddly minutes. What a sacrifice. And it took all the power of heaven and earth to get me to do it.

I miss you, Dad. I think a lot of us do.

2

LIFE AS HARDLY
LIFE AT ALL

Too Much

When I was an undergraduate, I was part of an experimental course. College students are often involved in educational experiments. But usually they don't find out about it until they are halfway into a course, at which time it becomes abundantly clear that the prof doesn't know where he's going, or the place he's going isn't worth getting to.

This course was different, however. We all knew it was an experiment and we were prepared for the consequences. Besides, it sounded fun. And short. It was a three-week intensive course in urban studies, the first half given over to traditional classroom instruction and the second designed as an urban plunge. The plan was to live in the city for a week and a half and study some of its people and institutions firsthand. And in this case, the plan was more than carried out.

On a typical day, we would wake up early in the morning, grab a quick bite to eat, and then be hustled off for a visit with gang leaders, social-service workers, urban-ministry leaders, city school teachers, urban pastors, and other assorted city types. From there we would

31

eat lunch with the homeless at a soup kitchen. Spend the next hour talking with members of the mayor's staff. Finish the afternoon trying to negotiate the city's public transportation system. Have dinner with the fishermen down at the wharf. And conclude the evening in the red-light district, talking with the prostitutes and avoiding pimps and drag queens. When we returned to our sleeping quarters, however, we were usually so keyed up by the day's events that we ended up talking half the night—sometimes about what we had seen, sometimes about what we hadn't seen but knew was there. It was an exhausting experience to say the least; an eye-opener without parallel at that time in my life.

One day especially stands out in my mind. After breakfast, we were scheduled to visit a large urban church, which specialized in counseling people with drug and relational problems. The ministry was called the "Drug and Sex Forum" and I remember giving that name a lot of thought before we got to the church. It sounded like an oxymoron for one thing. But the real problem was I couldn't get over the last word. *Forum*, I thought. *Ugh. Even "ministry" would be preferable to "forum." At least "ministry" connotes action. "Forum" sounds like an interminable string of words. And words, where drugs and sex are concerned, aren't likely to do the trick.* I didn't understand.

When we got to the church, we were greeted by a tall, lanky fellow with a sarcastic grin on his face and purpose in his gait. He quickly introduced himself as the director of the "Drug and Sex Forum" and told us to follow him downstairs. We were evangelicals, so we obediently complied, marching single file down the stairs, to a room in the basement of the church.

The room, however, was a surprise. It contained no chairs or furniture whatsoever. Instead, on the floor were strewn ten to fifteen large, overstuffed cushions, and on the walls there was nothing at all. No pictures, no clocks, no wallpaper, no evidence of anything except white paint. The only deviation from this pattern of blah was a dark window in the back wall of the room. And it seemed to be in hiding.

When we walked into the room, the director simply said, "Make yourselves comfortable," and then promptly left. That was strange, I thought, since he was supposed to be our host. But these were the late sixties and people were fond of doing things in strange ways. And so we did what college students are prone to do when they see cushions and are told to be comfortable—we went prone, stretched ourselves out on the floor and began telling jokes, laughing, and generally reducing our inhibitions a notch or two.

In due time, there was a noticeable change in the atmosphere of the room. Not only had we students been transformed into a more relaxed, free-spirited assembly, but the room itself had been transformed by the lowering of lights. Suddenly, without warning, the wall in front of us turned into a film screen, and we found ourselves watching a movie about a man brushing his teeth. At first, I thought this was one of those hygiene advertisements, except that there were no instructions accompanying the pictures. Only the sounds of the toothbrush moving ever so rapidly in some man's mouth.

As we watched, the film became increasingly bizarre. For one thing, the camera kept moving in closer and closer to the man's teeth, showing us far more of the fellow's oral cavity than anyone wanted to see. But eventually, the movie switched to other kinetic experiences, people rolling down hills, getting dressed, engaging in all kinds of active behavior. Finally, the movie ended, and I thought, *Good. Now the director will come out here and tell us about the deep psychological truths imbedded in the film, and how they relate to drugs, sex, and Age of Aquarius.* It was all starting to make sense.

Unfortunately, the director did not show himself. Instead, another film was projected onto the wall, this time about a bed (I knew that because it was cleverly entitled, "The Bed"), and it began with a scene of a four-poster bed careening down the side of a grass covered hill. When the bed reached the end of its slide, two people jumped out of the bed, and proceeded to run around the hillside in a Charlie Chaplin-ish fashion, laughing, cavorting, and generally having a grand old time of it. And, oh yes, they didn't have any clothes on.

I wasn't quick, as college students go, but it was fairly obvious to me that the movie had moved beyond bizarre and was becoming interesting. And pointed. And downright vulgar. A number of other students were apparently reaching the same conclusion and, within a short time, they began trickling out of the room. Finally, one of the braver souls among us stood up and announced, "I think this is wrong; let's get out of here." As he made his way for the door, everyone dragged themselves off their cushions and proceeded to follow him up the stairs.

Which meant that I was left all alone in the room, sitting there in the midst of fifteen lonesome cushions, in a church basement, watching a pornographic movie! Now I know what you're thinking. It was the same thing our leader was thinking when he came back into the room fifteen minutes later and said, "Gaede, get out here; we're leaving."

I considered this an insult, not to mention an embarrassment, and so quickly followed him up the stairs to where the rest of the group was waiting—waiting for their last member to make his ascent from hell. Before anyone could accuse me of poor taste, however, I launched into a moral tirade—not about the movie—but about their decision to leave the church. No doubt the moral tone of my comments was in part an effort to assuage my own guilt. But I felt the words deeply.

"We can't leave yet, you guys! Not until we have had a chance to talk with these people. Don't you want to know why they did this? Don't you want to know how this film relates to their drug-and-sex program? Besides, if we think it's wrong, don't we have an obligation to confront them with it?"

I was in high gear and I could tell that a number of them agreed with me. I could also tell, however, that others wanted to flee evil, and all appearances of evil, and they felt strongly that the right thing to do was to simply leave. They had a point.

Our leader came up with a compromise. "Okay. Those who want to talk with the director of the program may do so. The rest of us *good* Christians will go over to the museum. But let's all be at the museum in an hour."

My energy renewed, I quickly headed back down the stairs with four or five of my peers. Though I hadn't totally won the argument, I knew I had gained a great victory. Moments before, I had been the weakling; the one who couldn't resist temptation. Now, I was a tower of strength. The one who was willing to look the Devil straight in the eyes and ask, "Why?"

At least, that's what I hoped my peers were thinking. In my heart, however, it wasn't the Devil I expected to see in the basement. For I had long before come to the conclusion that something else was going on here. *These people aren't evil,* I told myself. *They're part of this church, aren't they? They are involved in a ministry that seeks to reach out to the needy people in the city. How could we simply assume they were immoral, therefore, and leave it at that? More than likely, they are using these films in their sex-and-drug ministry. Who knows, maybe the movies are a way of getting sex offenders to realize the destructiveness of their behavior. Maybe if we had stayed around a little longer, we would have discovered that the concluding film put everything into perspective, demonstrating the ghastly consequences of all that had preceded it.*

Those were my thoughts, anyway, as I leaped down the stairs. Either way, I figured I had a good chance of coming out on top. If these folks were wicked, I would debate them and show the others that I could be an advocate for righteousness' sake. But if they were sheep in wolves' clothing, I would come off as the mature one, who didn't jump to conclusions, and who could discover a diamond even in a dung heap.

When we reached the room in the church basement the film was over and the lights had been turned back on. The room was empty and, at first, we thought the people from the forum had left. Soon, however, we heard laughter coming from behind the window where the projector was located. As we approached the window, it became increasingly clear that the laughter had a certain edge to it; it didn't sound hearty, or merry, or particularly infectious. Indeed, it seemed rather rough. And pointed. And foreboding.

We continued walking toward the window, still opaque to our eyes but increasingly perceptible to our ears. *Whatever the laughter was about, it couldn't be good,* I thought to myself. One of us rapped on the glass and motioned for them to come out. In moments, the door flew open and the program director stepped into the room.

"What do you want?" he snapped, still snickering under his breath, and looking at us as if we were the most detestable creatures he had ever laid eyes on. It was obvious that our presence was no longer appreciated.

And to his question, it was obvious he did not desire an answer.

Nor was I prepared to give one. And in fact, I cannot remember my response, nor the responses of my companions. The conversation lasted for at least thirty minutes. I'm sure of that. Words were exchanged. Symbols were batted around. But the details of the dialogue remain a complete blur to me. What I do remember quite distinctly, however, was the meaning of the discussion. The implications remain crystal clear.

The laughter we had heard was indeed pointed; it was pointed at us. We learned that the men had determined that we were a bunch of naïve, immature, conservative Christians who needed a lesson about reality. And so they had taken it upon themselves to teach us about the real world, where drugs are a fact of life and sex is there for the taking. Our reaction to the films was, for them, merely confirmation that they were right. We weren't prepared for the facts of life. And they delighted in the knowledge that they had exposed us to them anyway.

And the films themselves? We were informed that the films were part of the forum's "educational program." Apparently, they had come to the conclusion that the best way to free people from their sexual hangups was to let everything hang out. And so they put both patients and therapists alike through an extensive program of graphic pornography. Pastors and counselors needed it, they said, so that they could be better prepared to deal with their clients who were wrestling with sexual problems. And clients needed it so they could give full expression to their sexual phobias.

Indeed, it turned out that the whole world needed it. We needed it because we hadn't been exposed to it yet. Teachers needed it because they needed to know what their students might be dealing with. Politicians needed it so they could come up with more enlightened policies. Religious people needed it so they could overcome their prudish inclinations. Everyone needed it, because ... well, because it is good to eat from the tree of the knowledge of good and evil. It will make you wise. And you will become like gods.

Too Little

When we left the church, I was shaken. Not simply because I was overwhelmed by evil, but because so much of what I had heard made sense. We were naïve, after all. That was demonstrated by the way we blindly walked into that basement without question and without much forethought.

But we were naïve in the way the director meant it as well. The city was not our home. Its pleasures and problems were no more real to us than the pictures on the evening news. And no doubt, he had a right to be appalled at our superficial understanding of his world.

It is true, as well, that good therapy depends on honest disclosure. No counselor can do his or her job without a good understanding of themselves. And few clients will be helped unless they are willing to explore the depths of their own feelings and emotions. Was it such a giant leap, then, from that need to the forum's film therapy? Might not a little disclosure of that kind be helpful? Aren't Christians a little too repressed, anyway? Couldn't my reaction be based more upon moral parochialism than good sense?

In every case, I had to answer "Yes." We were naïve. Therapy requires disclosure. And yes, Christians are sometimes repressed, parochial, and a whole lot more. And yet, at the conclusion of those sensible answers was a dark room. Full of cushions. Where people sat around. And enjoyed evil.

What is it about sin that enables it to exert such influence over reason? Or more to the point, why is the mind such a willing servant of evil? How is it possible to ask a series of reasonable questions, provide reasonable answers, and end up with such a wrong conclusion?

I had to ask that question again later that afternoon. For our next stop was a downtown hotel that had been converted into a "retirement center" for the elderly poor. I have always enjoyed being around the elderly, in part because I appreciate their honesty and lack of pretension, but also because I was blessed with a delightful gang of grandparents myself, who loved life and loved me as well. Consequently, I was looking forward to this part of our trip. It had to be an improvement on the morning.

When we arrived at the hotel, we were ushered into the lobby area and told to wait there until our guide arrived to show us around. After twiddling our thumbs for a short time, the group slowly began to break up, ambling to various corners of the lobby and poking our noses into a number of the side rooms. Nothing extraordinary was revealed by this exploration and so I finally decided to sit down beside an elderly gentleman and rest my weary feet.

"Good afternoon," I said politely.

No response. I sat there for a few minutes, looking around the lobby, acting as if I hadn't said anything, and trying to figure out my next move. Nothing brilliant came to mind, so I cleared my throat and I tried again.

"Uh ... good afternoon," I repeated.

Again, nothing. Why didn't he respond? I took a

quick glance at the man, hoping to find some clue to his behavior. But he was just sitting there. Staring straight ahead. Mouth closed. Unless he was a mannequin, his posture revealed little.

Maybe he didn't hear me, I thought to myself. *The elderly sometimes grow a little hard of hearing. I'll give it another shot.*

"Good afternoon," I said again, this time practically shouting in his ear.

"I heard you," came his quick reply. And then, almost as quickly, he lapsed back into studied silence.

It was a sharp rebuke, and I recoiled the minute I heard his words. Growing up in a small town, I had learned the rituals of rural civility and this was not among them. Indeed, even enemies would offer a polite "hello" in my hometown, though they might give you a sound thrashing thereafter. His "I heard you," to me, was hardly human. Or even animal. My dog at least responded when I called. This was calculated indifference. In that sense, maybe it was human—but not humane.

I sat motionless for a few more minutes trying to absorb the man's blow and prepare for a quick departure at the same time. Finally, I took a deep breath and lifted myself off the bench. When I reached full height, I looked down at the old man just in time to see his eyes trying to catch mine.

"Finally leaving, are you?" he said matter-of-factly. "You're slower than most."

I looked at him for a few seconds, not knowing whether to respond or continue along with my departure plan. My heart said, "Keep moving. You don't need this fellow today." But curiosity wrested control of my tongue.

"What do you mean?" I said, thinking how stupid it sounded, and how dangerous, given this fellow's rapier communication skills.

"Most people leave after the first 'hello,'" he said nonchalantly. "A few will try it a second time. But no one goes for three. You from a small town or somethin'?"

The last comment was another jab. But when he said it his eyes brightened just a bit. And for the first time I knew I had a human being on my hands. "Small town," I said as I eased back onto the seat beside him. "And I'm not used to such ... uh ... behavior from ... uh—"

"An old man?" he intruded, finishing my sentence for me. "Well that's just fine because I'm not much used to behavior of any kind from young kids these days. ..."
He paused for a moment, and I could tell that he was trying to decide whether to explain himself or take another dive below sea level. He changed the subject instead.

"What are you kids doin' around here today anyway? Studyin' old men or somethin'? Tryin' to find out what kind of people are stupid enough to live in a rattrap like this?"

"Well, actually ..." and, then, as I was trying to formulate an answer, it dawned on me that he was exactly correct, for the second time. We didn't use quite the same terms to describe our activity, of course. We thought of our adventure as an attempt to understand the conditions of the elderly poor, not simply study them. But I had to admit, the difference between the two was largely euphemistic. And from the perspective of the old man, irrelevant.

"Well ... uh ... we're studying the city," I said quickly. "But ... why did you say before that you weren't used to any kind of behavior from kids?"

"Because I don't see very many. ..." And as he talked his voice began to fade and his eyes began to take on the look of incommunicado I had observed before. I thought I was going to lose him again.

"But ... what about your grandchildren? Don't you

get to see them once in a while?" I implored, hoping to turn his mind to brighter thoughts.

He continued to stare straight ahead. And then, ever so gently, shook his head from side-to-side.

"Oh," I responded. "I'm sorry. I just assumed you had grandchildren. That was stupid of me. I grew up in a fairly large—"

"I have grandchildren," he interrupted. "At least, I think I still do. I had four children myself, and I know all of them got married—some more than once. They have children too. I used to see them when they were little. When Mary was still alive, and we were livin' in the outside world. But I don't see them anymore. I used to get letters once in a while. Sometimes they would send pictures. But letters don't come very often now. Nothin' comes much anymore. Nothin' and nobody." He paused for a moment. ". . . And I don't much care anymore, you know?"

It was a lie. And in the next hour I was to learn just how much he cared and how painful his life had become as a result. Like many who are elderly, his problems began a few years after retirement, when his wife died, and he was left alone to fend for himself. For a while, he managed fairly well, living off a modest savings account and social security. Eventually, however, his income was outstripped by inflation, and he ended up using most of his savings to pay for his apartment. His health also deteriorated during this time (arthritis) and he found it increasingly difficult to shop, walk the stairs, and keep his apartment clean.

Most of his children had moved away by this time and the only one he had any personal contact with was a son in a nearby suburb. Periodically, when his son had business in the city, he would drop by to say hello. But the contacts became more and more infrequent as the years rolled along. This didn't bother him too much, he said, because he had friends living in the area. Besides, he confessed, he had never been that close to his children. "Mary raised them," he would say, "and when she died, we didn't have much of a reason to be together anymore."

One of the last times he saw his son was after he took a bad fall down the apartment stairs. He was hospitalized for a few days, and apparently the doctor called his son, concerned about the attention his dad would need during convalescence. His son was concerned as well. And during the few days his father was in the hospital, he managed to secure a spot for him at the "retirement center," move all of his belongings out of his apartment, and liquidate his savings account. The old man was informed of these actions on the day he was released from the hospital, and that evening he found himself sitting in a small hotel room in an alien part of the city, stripped of his friends, neighborhood, and assets. He had never felt so alone in his whole life.

He would get used to the feeling, however. In fact, during his ten years in the retirement center, he said his feelings of loneliness had only grown worse. He found it difficult to make friends. He couldn't take walks outside because the neighborhood was unsafe—especially for the elderly, who are easy prey for muggers and thieves. He loathed his room, which was small, windowless, and without toilet facilities. He had absolutely no responsibilities (even his finances were taken care of by the center). He was often cold and always hungry. And with each passing year, he grew more and more bitter toward his children, who had placed him there and then promptly cut off all contact with him. In essence, he said, his children had imprisoned him.

"For what?" he kept asking. "For what? What did I do to earn this anyway? I wasn't a great father, I'll admit that. I was gone too much and there were many years when I worked two jobs at once. But I was only trying to feed my family. Is that a crime? Do they put you in jail for working too hard these days, for crying out loud? Or was it Mary's fault for dying? Is that where I went wrong? I don't know. I just don't know. . . ."

And then the faraway look would return, and I would find myself making some silly comment or reaching for one more question, just to bring him back to life. It was almost as if I was holding a dying man in my arms, who was trying to decide whether or not to give in to his fate. I would slap him on the face with my persistent questioning, and he would respond with a burst of consciousness. But the responses kept getting shorter. And with every retort, he seemed to find less and less reason to go on living.

In due time, our tour guide leader arrived and I had the unpleasant task of bidding the old man good-bye. I realized, as I searched my vocabulary for the right words to say, that I didn't even know his name. Nor he, mine.

"I have to go now," I said apologetically. "Thanks for talking to me. I want you to know that I'll be praying for you. . . ." I bit my tongue. The words sounded trite and condescending. By what right does a twenty-year-old kid offer to intercede with God on behalf of an old man? Besides I couldn't pray for him; I didn't even know his name.

"My name is Stan, by the way. I—"

"That's good," he interrupted, not giving me time to ask his name.

"My name?" I responded, somewhat perplexed.

"That you're going to pray for me," he said. "That's good. That's all I've got, you know."

I was dumbfounded. Nothing in his conversation remotely suggested that he was a religious man. And it seemed inconceivable to me that a Christian would find himself in this predicament.

"Are you a Christian?" he asked, pulling out a tender tone that I had not heard up to that time.

I nodded. "Yes, I am. . . ." And then I hesitated asking, because I was afraid of the answer. "Are you?"

"Well," he said, pausing for just a moment, "I've accepted Jesus as my Savior. Many times, in fact. So I guess, if that's what it takes, I am. Mary was a good Christian, I'll tell you that. And she took the kids to church every Sunday, whether I was workin' or not. Truth is, she loved the Lord more than me. But I never minded cause the Lord gave her plenty of love to go around, and I sure as the world got my share. . . . She was a good woman, Mary was. A mighty good woman. . . ."

And then, when I thought I had lost him again, "But I haven't been feelin' like a very good man of late. And to be honest with you, I'm not all that sure that God still loves me. But . . . that's my hope, isn't it? And that's why I appreciate you prayin' for me."

Words completely fail me at times like these. My throat grows thick and my mind turns to mush. I knew I should have offered him some words of encouragement. I wanted to tell him that he *was* loved. That God's love was not merely a hope, but a reality. But I also realized that he saw no evidence of that love in his present circumstances. He had been abandoned by his own flesh and blood, and left to wither away in an old building with a lot of other old people. In the light of such evidence, the assurances of a twenty-year-old kid seemed a paltry thing indeed.

I made a stab at it, nevertheless. And my last memories are those of an old man, looking up at me, wanting to believe that God still loved him. And me, awkwardly trying to say good-bye, telling him I would pray for him, and encouraging him not to lose faith in a good and loving God. It's a painful memory to this day.

When I caught up with the other students, they were

just getting on the elevator. I stepped in as the doors were about to close, pushing the door's edge to restrain its pincer movement. It had no effect, and I had to leap forward to avoid being pulverized. And I thought of the old man, with his arthritis, trying to get on the elevator.

We stopped at the twenty-first floor, for no particular reason, and began walking down one of the halls. The light was very dim, so it was hard to see, but some things were obvious even in the dark. The carpet on the floor was tattered and dirty, for one thing. And the plaster on the walls was deteriorating for another. But the most striking feature of the hall was the pungent smell of urine, made mordant by the hot stagnant air. And I thought of the old man, waking up in the middle of the night with a full bladder, trying to negotiate the corridor so he could use the bathroom at the end of the hall.

The guide opened up one of the rooms and only a few of us stepped inside. Only a few of us could. It was cleaner than the hall but not as large, having space for a small bed, a lamp stand, one chair, and a small sink. There were no windows. No decorations. And no telephone.

"Don't they have phones?" one of the students asked incredulously. "What happens in an emergency? What happens if they're sick and can't come down for a meal? How can they let anyone know?"

"They can have a telephone," the guide responded, "but they have to pay for it themselves. Most of them are living on social security, however, and that just barely covers their rent here. So almost no one has a phone. As far as sickness is concerned, that's a problem. Usually, someone will notice if meals are being missed, and then a staff member will go up to check it out. But a lot of people miss meals periodically, so it takes a little while before we know there's a problem."

"A little while?" another student repeated questioningly.

"Yes," the guide went on breezily. "Sometimes it takes a day or two before we realize that someone's not coming down for meals. That's especially bad if they're dead. You don't want to walk in a room when someone's been dead for two or three days! Any more questions?"

No. No more questions. Just a thought. Of an old man, living out the last hours of his life in a small stuffy room. Without friends or family or even a staff member by his side. Without the knowledge that his body will be properly cared for after his death. An old man. Totally and completely alone. And wondering if he is without the love of the Lord as well.

And again, just as in the morning, I was left with the question, why? Why do children find it so easy to abandon their parents at the time they are needed the most? Why is it that a "retirement center" can be more concerned about a dead man's stench than a live man's well-being? Why is it that in a society where ninety percent of the population say they believe in God, so many find it a burden to keep the fourth commandment?

There are reasons, of course, just as there were reasons why the Drug and Sex Forum dispensed pornography: Children will tell you that they are too busy with their own families and careers to take on additional responsibility for their elderly parents. Retirement centers will say that they don't have the money to invest in cleaning agents, staff training, and telephones. And a nation will argue that the fourth commandment wasn't designed for an urbanized, industrialized society like ours.

But at the end of all these good reasons there remains an old man. Sitting in his room. Alone. As surely the product of evil as anything ever imagined by the purveyors of smut.

Just Right

An encounter such as I had in San Francisco leaves one feeling discouraged and depressed. It reminds us that life is difficult. And that all too often, it doesn't even seem particularly fair. It is the story of Job all over again, people getting worse than they deserve and everyone else left standing around asking why.

But the story of Job doesn't end in defeat. And we miss the mark if we only notice the victories of the Evil One. Indeed, though life presents us with many perplexities and tragedies, it seems to be woven together by an underlying thread of justice. Evildoers do, in time, reap the whirlwind. And those who forget this equation are doomed to relearn it the hard way.

A friend told me a story recently that reminded me of that fact. I can't vouch for its veracity, but I'll share it with you anyway. The truth of the story is not dependent on the details.

The story begins and ends in a high-rise parking lot in downtown Boston. For those of you who haven't been entertained by Boston traffic lately, let me simply say that Bostonians are without doubt the worst drivers in

North America. Boston roads are the most confusing.
Boston policemen are the least conscious (I'm tempted to
stop there) of traffic regulations and the least inclined to
enforce those of which they inadvertently become aware.
Boston parking spaces are the rarest of commodities. And
as a result, Boston parking lots are the most expensive
pieces of real estate imaginable, fetching fees that are
astonishing to even the most hardened urbanite. As you
can imagine, then, people who find themselves in a
Boston parking lot are not generally the most congenial
folks in the world.

This was demonstrated quite pointedly, recently,
when a young man in a sports car literally stole a parking
place right out from under the nose of a little old lady.
Apparently, the lady was quite elderly, and she was
taking her time getting her enormously expensive Mercedes into one of the few vacant parking spaces in the
entire building. Just as she was about to enter the space,
however, a young fellow in a snazzy, new sports car
dashed in front of her, cut her off, and whipped his car
into the space she had assumed was hers.

Well, needless to say, the lady was nonplussed. But
to make matters worse, when the young man got out of
his car, he casually strode by the old woman's car, peered
into her window, broke into a huge grin and quipped,
"You can do that when you're young and fast, you
know." And off he went for a pleasant day in Boston.

The man was about halfway down the stairs, however, when he heard a tremendous crash in the parking
lot above. Being a curious chap, he reversed course and
headed back up the stairs to inspect the damage. On his
way up, he heard a second crash, which sounded
remarkably similar to the first and raised his curiosity
level even higher. When he arrived at the top of the
stairs, he was greeted not only with a third crash but with
the surprise of his life: The little old lady was carefully

and methodically ramming her Mercedes into his sports car, moving it a foot or two with each crack, and eventually dislodging it from the parking space entirely. Once the space was again vacant, she calmly filled it with her own car and reclaimed the site for herself.

By this time, of course, the young man was practically apoplectic. He raced up to the old lady, hurling all sorts of insults, epithets, and questions her way, desperately trying to comprehend the reason for her behavior. The old lady, however, paid absolutely no attention to him whatsoever. She just continued her casual pace, putting on a little more lipstick, fluffing her hair a bit, adjusting her coat and, in due time, opening the door and getting out of the car. Once outside, she again adjusted her apparel, made sure the car was locked and composed herself for a second time. And then, at last, when everything was in place and she was prepared to go, she looked the young man straight in the eye: "You can do that when you're old and rich, you know," she said. And off she went for a pleasant day in Boston.

3

LIFE AS A
STORY

Discretion

Privacy is a problem when you're dating, especially when you're trying to be discreet. Two types of couples have no privacy problems at all: those whose relationship is entirely cerebral and those whose relationship is entirely physical. Cerebral couples don't care if anyone sees them. And physical couples don't care about discretion. Everyone else must engage in the delicate art of finding time alone while maintaining standards of decency and decorum.

Judy and I were definitely in the "everyone else" category. And I looked at the cerebral or physical types with great incredulity. And maybe even some envy. How could they possibly carry on like that, I wondered? Were they brave? Or stupid? Or was there just something wrong with the equipment? I couldn't understand it.

Take the cerebral types, for example. How can two people of the opposite sex—who are attracted to each other, considering marriage, and who have no prior history at Johns Hopkins—carry on a wholly dispassionate relationship? I am not talking about platonic friendships between men and women, mind you. That I

53

understand. I mean those couples who think of themselves as "couples," who believe they are developing a deeper relationship, and who in some cases are engaged. How do they carry on as if hormones don't exist?

"Good morning, dear. How are you?"

"Quite good, actually. Had a wonderful sleep. Life seems quite grand today, doesn't it?"

"Oh yes, quite. Only this morning, I had the good fortune to spot a Red Nose-hair Blue Bird strutting along my windowsill. What a marvelous creature he is. Sometimes I think the mystery of the universe is contained in that one little hair."

"Oh, bravo. Indeed. Quite. Rather . . ."

Watching couples like that, I vacillate between thinking they are vastly superior beings or perhaps vastly superior liars. I mean, do they really carry on like this in all honesty? Is the Red Nose-hair Blue Bird really the light of their life, deserving half the morning for conversation and contemplation? Or is it all a cover-up for deeply repressed emotions—a lovely cosmetic, conveniently hiding the fact that they would both like to tear each other's clothes off? Who knows? Viennese psychoanalysts would assume the latter, but maybe they're just a bunch of repressed Red Nose-hair Blue Bird lovers themselves.

On the other hand, I don't understand Velcro couples either. Especially the ones who plop down in the middle of some public space and practice knot tying with their bodies. Some people manage to ignore such couples, but I cannot. I am too amazed it's happening not to notice and too interested in the outcome to avert my eyes. It is different, of course, when one stumbles across a couple embracing behind a big oak tree in the park. There one feels like an intruder, barging into a failed attempt at privacy. But when there is no attempt at all, it is I who feel taken advantage of. And I think it's important to keep a wary eye on one's exploiters.

The question remains: Why do some couples intertwine in public? In the sixties, the obvious answer would have been, if it feels good do it. If others are offended, that's their problem. This sounded good, but it ran smack into another value of the sixties, community. The question became, do we care about others or don't we? If we do, then why would we want to deliberately offend them, especially when it's quite easy not to? What this brought to light was that many people who were doing the offending were not simply trying to "do their own thing," but they were trying to be provocative. Their offensiveness was deliberate, motivated out of social protest or personal spite.

I had to consider, then, the possibility that intertwining couples, as children of the sixties, were being deliberately offensive. But that hardly fit the Velcro couples that I knew. They were the least likely to engage in social protest, not the most likely, and on the personal level they were often quiet and even shy. So provocation seemed out of the question as a motivation, unless it was deeply subliminal. (Again, the Viennese psychoanalyst would have something to say; but again, I don't really care.)

What I concluded, then, was that the Velcro phenomenon was rooted in one of two possibilities. The first was naïveté. Some couples, I came to believe, were just dumb. They liked each other. They had hormones. And that was as much as they could comprehend. Time, place, and propriety simply didn't enter into their calculations. Given their affections, if they were together, they went into action. That was all there was to it.

The second possibility is what I call *couplism*. Couplism is like any other -isms (hedonism, fascism, individualism) in that it subordinates all other interests to one, which in this case is the couple. In other words, for the Velcro couple, the world begins and ends with them. Nothing else matters. College, family, church, nation—they are of little concern, except as means to an end. And the end is coupledom.

The college, for example, is convenient for geographical reasons because it provides a place to be a couple. But it is a bother too because it requires study, class attendance, and separate living quarters. For the couple, the answers to these problems are as follows: study, if done at all, is done together. Classes, if attended, are attended together. And sleeping ... well, sleeping hardly occurs at all: one retires to one's room only when it is essential, either out of sheer exhaustion or (in those days) because college policy says you must.

All of this analysis did nothing to help my condition, of course. It did make me feel a little better, knowing that I was not the victim of naïveté, couple-centrism, or inactive hormones. But it still left Judy and me with a problem. Our relationship was neither totally physical nor entirely cerebral. We were, like most other couples, trying to achieve some balance in our lives. And trying to do it discreetly. The question remained, how?

Now I had one advantage over many other college students: I had a car. Growing up on a farm, one of the first things one learns is how to drive. First, a neighbor's horse or a large dog. Then a bicycle. Then a go-cart. Then a small Ford tractor. Then a big John Deere (now we're talking work). Then a pick-up. And finally, at around age ten, a car. Driving is a farm boy's lifeline to civilization, the only thing that prevents farm disease. So even the poorest of rural lads tries not to live without a car of his own.

But away at college, the car had a different function. It was a means of escape. And there is no end to the number of things one wants to escape from in college:

dorms, studies, rules, wash . . . the list goes on and on. At any given moment in time, I could come up with at least fifty reasons why I should just get in my car and drive. But when you are a couple, the primary thing you wish to escape is publicity. And the number-one objective is privacy. Which means that you are constantly in search of good parking spots. And they seem constantly to be alluding you.

I had one spot that was just fabulous. On a bluff overlooking the city, only a bimbo (or is it bimba?) would have failed to fall in love with me there. I even thought I was pretty great there. And then, wouldn't you know it, Joe Preacher from down the hall discovers the same spot and sits there night after night with his girlfriend. The sad thing was, they were a cerebral couple. Which meant they weren't using the spot to its full potential (I hate waste). But it also meant that they had lots of opportunity to look around and see what other couples were up to. Needless to say, I scratched that spot off my list in a hurry. But I had a deep sense of loss doing it.

The really difficult evenings were when you only had about thirty minutes between the end of a movie downtown and the curfew back at the college. Since it took ten to fifteen minutes to drive back to campus, one had at most twenty minutes to find a good parking place, say something meaningful, and shoot a few lippies. And all of this depended on the fact that the parking place was on a direct route from the theater to the campus. I was aware of very few such places, however, and the ones I knew about were also known by the town's entire college population; one could get more privacy in front of the administration building. So on such evenings, things could get pretty desperate.

It was on just such an evening that I made a wonderful discovery. We were returning to campus after a movie, and as usual, we only had about fifteen minutes before Judy had to be in. I had pretty much given up on the possibility of privacy that evening, and so we just headed straight back to the college. When we got to the college gate, however, I couldn't bear the thought of returning early and so, instead of turning into the campus, I drove right past the gate and soon found myself winding up the hill behind the college.

Surprising as it may seem, I had never been up that hill before. Everyday, I could look at Mountain Mama from my perch in the library. It was beautiful, especially during the greenest months, and I often admired the variety of plants and shrubs that glazed it slopes. But it never dawned on me that it might be a place I would want to park. It was filled with large estates, for one thing, and I assumed it was all private property. But it also seemed much too close to campus to contain a good parking spot. If there was one, everyone would know about it. I had heard nothing so just assumed it was off limits.

Boy was I wrong. As we wound up the mountain, I was confronted with every romantic's dream. Beautiful scenery. Periodic rest stops. And best of all, silence. No cars, no people, no distractions of any kind. Just God, his lovely creation, and us. I couldn't believe my good fortune. I pulled off the side of the road and stopped the motor. Looking at my watch, I could see that we had 13 minutes and 45.03 seconds for meaningful conversation plus.

We were in the process of finding meaning when I noticed a light reflecting off of my rearview mirror. I assumed it was a passing car and didn't pay too much attention; we were quite a distance off the road and I doubted the driver would even notice us. I began to pay attention, however, when the light didn't pass but only grew brighter. And my attention meter went right off the end of the scale when the light stopped directly behind us and was fortified by the color red.

Judy must have thought it was the end of the world because she jerked her head around so quickly, I thought my lower lip would end up in the back seat. She did manage to get my head turned in the right direction, however, and I was finally able to see the full extent of our predicament. The light belonged to a policeman, and the officer was already walking over to my side of the car. My first thought was that I would get out and save the man a few steps. That way he could then see that I was sober, fully dressed, and had short hair, all of which were marks of obedience in those days. Besides, I thought to myself, we weren't doing anything wrong. He just needs to see that we're a couple of regular kids, minding our own business.

Unfortunately, Judy must have had the same idea because we both leaped from the car at the same time. Stunned by this turn of events, I looked over at Judy and then back to the officer, who was at that moment reaching for something from his side. I stopped dead in my tracks, wondering if I soon would be, and watched as the policeman's hand found its object, raised it in my direction, and then shot a blot of light squarely into my eyes.

"May I see your license, young man," he said sternly.

Relieved but now partly blind, I began fumbling around in my back pocket for my billfold. Judy must have decided I needed help, because instead of getting back in the car or smiling politely at the officer or disappearing under the floorboard, she suddenly found her voice.

"I'm sixteen years old!" she yelled out in a strong but quavering voice, as if she were somewhat proud and somewhat surprised.

I was, of course, totally dumbfounded. *Sixteen!* What in the world was she talking about! She's nineteen, going on twenty. A college sophomore. A full-grown, twice-born, soon-to-be-married woman. So why in the world was she telling Quickdraw that she was sixteen?

I didn't brood over this question long because it suddenly dawned on me that I was in a rather precarious position. The policeman, now inspecting my license, was soon to discover that I was twenty-one years old. Judy, on the other hand, who looked young, whose voice was quavering, and who leaped from the car like an escaped convict, was claiming to be just sixteen. It didn't take a lot of marbles to figure out what was going in the officer's mind.

"Judy," I said pleadingly, "you are *not* sixteen."

Judy, however, had said as much as she was going to say. She just stood their stoically, biting her lip, and looking at me. And I? Well, I stood there too. Waiting to be arrested for child abuse. Knowing that whatever career lay before me ... well, it didn't lay before me anymore. And wondering why I couldn't be satisfied contemplating the wonders of the Red Nose-hair Blue Bird.

Meaning

Two questions arise from the last chapter. First, what happened? And second, what's the point? The first question is the easiest. Because the officer simply looked at my license, ignored Judy's comment, and told the two of us to get lost. Which we did posthaste never to return again. Question number two is a bit more difficult. What was the meaning behind the last chapter? What was my purpose in writing it, anyway?

There are some things I learned from the experience, certainly. Some things about myself, about couples, and most assuredly about Judy. For example, this was the first time I discovered that I'm a better actor than Judy. When caught by the policeman, my first inclination was to perform my way through it. To act innocent and obedient, and hope the policeman would just tell us to move along. Judy was hoping for the same outcome but, instead of acting her way through the situation, she simply blurted out what she thought was the quintessential point—that she was over sixteen years old. She didn't say "over," of course, which means she not only failed to act naturally, she also failed to make her point. But her intentions were honorable.

I have thought long and hard about Judy's inability to act, by the way, and I have come to two possible conclusions. The first is that she's far more honest than I am, and indeed, more honest than anyone I know. She can't hide anything because she can't be anything other than herself. I, on the other hand, have dreamed of being many things during my lifetime, from cop, to cowboy, to president. Each of these dreams required that I suppress certain facts about myself—that I'm not particularly courageous or brave, for instance—and invent others. Though I no longer fantasize about such things, all that dreaming was good exercise. It taught me how to act. And it proved to be a wonderful training ground for my eventual career as a professor.

There is a second possibility, however, which must be given equal consideration. Judy was raised in the suburbs of Los Angeles and I was raised on a farm. You may think that L.A., being near Hollywood, is the perfect breeding ground for actors. But that's not true. Indeed, the farm is much more fertile soil for thespians.

The way I see it, farming offers something that suburbia does not—time. Let's face it, a lot of farming is sitting around and doing nothing. Don't get me wrong, sometimes the farmer toils harder than anyone, as all spade workers know. But other times you just have to sit there, while the tractor goes back and forth. Or stand there till the water reaches the end of the row. It is important work but it is immensely boring. The flip side of boredom, though, is time. Time to contemplate. Time to think. Time to dream. My dad used this time to think, and thus he excelled in wisdom. A friend used this time to sing, and thus be became a great musician. I used the time to dream, and thus became a great actor—or at least, as great an actor as the equipment would allow.

Judy, on the other hand, grew up in Los Angeles where there is no time, or more precisely, where there is always opportunity. If you feel like swimming, you swim. If you feel like shopping, you shop. Whatever it is you want to do, you generally can do. Weather is rarely an impediment. And affluence seems to be the order of the day. All of which means there are fewer constraints on one's behavior. Fewer times, that is, when one has to sit and do nothing. Fewer times to simply wait and dream.

I am not saying that it is better to grow up on a farm than in L.A. If "by their fruit you shall know them," and Judy and I represent the fruit of L.A. and the farm, respectively, then suburbia wins hands down. But I do think there are advantages to growing up disadvantaged. And theater arts may be one of them.

So we could conclude that I learned some important information about Judy and myself from this encounter. But that hardly seems worth a chapter, does it? I also learned about the difficulty of being discreet, especially in the area of romance. But again, that scarcely seems like a bold revelation. Who hasn't stolen a kiss, only to be caught red-handed in the process? Or just as discouraging, who hasn't sat there like an idiot while a golden opportunity for theft passes right by? We all find discretion difficult. That's why we call its attainment virtuous.

Of course, upon reflection, I also learned a bit about being a couple. And I suppose that's worth something. When you think about it, you'll discover that I mostly learned what I didn't understand. Certainly, that is the case for the cerebral couple; their actions—or nonactions, to be precise—remain totally baffling to me to this day. But even my theories of the Velcro phenomenon are less than satisfying. They had the benefit of making me look smart for not participating in Velcroism, but they hardly explained the phenomenon. And besides, who cares about coupledom anyway? As a sport, quite a few. As a discipline, zip.

So the mystery of this chapter remains. Why include it? If there is no purpose, if there is no deeper meaning, why even bring it up?

I suppose, then, that it's time I made a confession: I told the story about Judy and the cop because . . . well, because I think it's funny. And I discussed coupledom simply because I think it's interesting. And that's all there is to it. Funny and interesting, period. No deeper meaning. No hidden purpose. No underlying truth. Just stories. And a bit of rumination. Nothing more.

But nothing less. And that's the point, if there must be one. It's enjoyable to figure out why people do things. And it's fun to tell stories. Those are two qualities that separate us from the rest of God's creation. They are uniquely human traits. And for that reason—because they are gifts of the Creator—they do not always have to be employed to uncover some deeper meaning. Every analysis doesn't have to lead to profound truth. Every story doesn't need to make a point. They have a God-given goodness to them. And that goodness can stand on its own.

I say all of this because I think that fact is sometimes missed by modern Christians. And I miss it myself, once in a while. This was brought home to me recently while participating in a Bible-study group. We were going through the book of Genesis and we came to the story of the Tower of Babel. I like that incident because I think it reveals a good deal about human nature and its collision course with God. Consequently, I began verbalizing my interpretation, waxing on and on about the deeper meaning behind the story.

When I had finally finished my interpretation, a friend in the Bible study—who happens to be a biblical scholar and first-rank theologian, no less—impolitely said, "You could be right. It could mean all of that. But on the other hand, it could simply be an explanation for the diversity of languages in the world."

I was flabbergasted. Not by his impertinence (which I have gotten used to by now and take as a mark of endearment) but by his no-nonsense interpretation of the story. Could he be right? Could this story be merely what it seems to be on the surface, an account of language diversity? It was almost inconceivable to me that that might be all there was to it. Even though that was the most obvious interpretation. And even though that was probably how many Israelites understood it in the first place.

The point here is not that this is the best interpretation of the Tower of Babel. I still don't think it is—I'm stubborn regardless of who makes me look foolish—and I remain convinced that it is a rich vein that can be mined for more than what lies on the surface. But what intrigues me is my own compulsion to find deeper meanings. And even more important, the fact that I had never come across my friend's interpretation in forty years of church services, Bible studies, chapels, etc. Why not?

The answer, I suspect, contains a rough mixture of good and bad. On the good side, Christians take the Bible seriously. It is God's Word, after all. It is there for our instruction and nurture, and we want to learn all we can from it. We have seen the Bible denuded by Enlightenment and post-modern thinking. Indeed, we have seen the inherent meaninglessness of modern thought itself. And we are not about to let either of those two trends affect our thinking, either about the Bible or about life. We look for deeper meaning because of what we know and because of what we are reacting against.

On the negative side, however, I think we sometimes have trouble living with our own ignorance. And if there is anything stories and investigations lead to, it is the limits of our own understanding. A good story is like a good science project: Every discovery leads to multiple unknowns. That is why *good* stories can be told again and again. Because they are always fresh, always full of new horizons and images never seen before. That is why *good* science leads to humility. Because with every revelation, there is the deeper revelation of how little the scientist really knows. (The fact that many modern writers and scientists remain arrogant only goes to show how little *good* writing and research gets done these days.)

Modern Christians seem to have trouble with mystery, with the fact that "we see through a glass darkly." Maybe it's because we're defensive about our faith in an age of skepticism. Maybe it's because we've been influenced more by Greece than Israel. Whatever the cause, we seem to possess an overriding need to have everything wrapped up. We are uncomfortable saying, "I don't know." We are compelled to find deeper meanings.

As a result, we sometimes miss the joy in a story. Or the fun in a research project. We read a great novel and feel guilty for wasting time. If asked, we are compelled to justify such indulgence by reiterating all the hidden truths in the story, when in truth we just had a good time. We get overinvolved in our child's homework project and spend the evening tracking down the etymology of words or the workings of the solar system, and we deride ourselves for wasting an evening on a curiosity. "Think of all the work we could have gotten done," we say. Or all the sleep we missed out on.

Time is precious. And work has its place. But so does story telling and curiosity following. And their value does not rest on their ability to unlock the secrets of the universe or cure an incurable disease, though sometimes they can do both. Their value comes from the Creator, who honored our curiosity by putting us in a universe teaming with questions, who honored our stories by using them to communicate his very Word.

True, our curiosity can lead to disobedience. And passions inflamed by stories can be ill used. We live in a fallen world. And like all of God's good gifts, these too can be spent on evil. And will be. As will time and work and play and anything else humans have the capacity for doing.

But let's not forget that it was God who made us storytellers in the first place, that it was he who gave us inquiring minds. We say of the disobedience of Adam and Eve that their curiosity got the best of them. But we lie. It was their pride—their desire to rival God—that got them in trouble. And the same thing holds true for us today. If our pride gets ahold of God's gifts, the gift will always be abused. But the answer is not to reject the gift and thereby insult the Giver. It is rather to enjoy the gift and thank the Giver.

And use it. Whether we find deeper meaning or not.

4

LIFE AS A
LOVER

Desire

Like every good love story, ours began on our wedding day. I don't mean that Judy and I fell in love on our wedding day. We had been smitten by the love bug much earlier than that. But the drama of living with the one you love began on that day, along with all the privileges and responsibilities attendant to it.

In my experience, weddings are nearly always delightful events. Good weather usually prevails. Women are rarely as beautiful. And people are incomparably gracious and in good humor. Men, of course, often grouse about having to go to weddings—I do it myself—but that attitude can't possibly have anything to do with the facts. Most men have a rollicking good time at weddings. Kissing women they shouldn't kiss. And consuming quantities of food previously thought unimaginable.

Anyway, our wedding day was of the usual kind, which means it was fabulous. Men, women, weather, and ambience all cooperated splendidly. The ceremony itself went well, culminating in a glorious celebration of our love for one another. No doubt about it, we had a great time.

Nevertheless, in spite of my affection for weddings, I must tell you, in all honesty, that I was rather more interested in the honeymoon than the nuptial rites. I may have been unusual in this regard, I don't know. But as we headed off from church that day, my mind was focused not so much on the past, but the possibilities inherent in the future. And the future was sitting right beside me, looking absolutely radiant.

We have a cocker spaniel who, when about to receive a scrumptious morsel, stands at our feet, tail wagging at blinding speed and saliva drooling out of the edges of her mouth. It is not a pretty sight but it certainly communicates her feelings. Well, I have no doubt that, as we left the church that evening, I resembled our cocker spaniel.

It took us a little over an hour to reach our honeymoon suite in Newport Beach, California. Actually, we could have gotten there sooner, but we decided to stop at a drive-in for a hamburger first. I can't for the life of me explain why—after consuming all those goodies at our wedding reception—we were still hungry. But we were. And I suppose it says something about our priorities that we were willing to satisfy our palates before proceeding to the main event. (Actually, that part makes more sense to me the older I get—but that's another story.)

When we arrived at the inn, everything was perfect. I had spent a good deal of time selecting our honeymoon suite, previewing not only the inn but the precise room we would be occupying. When we arrived, therefore, the suite was waiting for us, festooned with flowers, chocolates, and other amenities appropriate for the occasion. The room itself was lovely, with a balcony overlooking the bay and a bed large enough to get lost in (which was not my intention, certainly).

Forgive me for digressing at this point, but sociologists stress that human beings learn proper behavior through socialization; they aren't born with it. Children learn to eat ice cream with a spoon rather than a knife, not because it comes naturally, but through the instruction and example of parents. Once in a while, however, humans find themselves in circumstances for which they have had little preparation and virtually no previous experience. A honeymoon, for example. If sociologists are correct, such circumstances ought to be more than a bit problematic, eliciting a great deal of anxiety and insecurity.

Sociologists are correct. Until the moment we stepped into the room, all of my energy had been spent preparing the accoutrements of the occasion—transportation, room, flowers, etc. What I had not thought too much about, however, were the details of the occasion itself. I don't mean by this that I was ill-prepared for the main event, by the way. About that, there had been no shortage of imagination or forethought. What I had not given much thought to was the period of time between the threshold maneuver and the first nibble of an earlobe. What do you do anyway? Sit down for a chat about the weather? Admire the stucco on the ceiling? Take a shower? What is appropriate behavior in such circumstances? I hadn't the foggiest idea.

If I remember correctly, we did all of the above. I'm not sure, however, because I spent the entire time feeling insecure, lost, and totally out of sync with the world. Before we walked into the room, I was goal-directed, confident, and in control. After that, all sense of direction and purpose vanished. Poof! I do recall fumbling around in my suitcase, hanging up clothes, and eventually putting on my pajamas. What my poor bride was doing or thinking during my stupor, I have no idea. No doubt on her knees before her Creator, inquiring as to how she had gotten herself into this mess in the first place.

My first clear remembrance of Judy is of her sauntering out of the bathroom in a gorgeous white negligee, calm, self-assured, and (quite unbelievably) in pursuit of me. No man has ever been more thoroughly and undeservedly rescued from self-destruction. I responded by instinct rather than forethought, and soon I was lost in the arms of the one I loved. From hell to heaven in less than a nanosecond.

Or so I thought. As it turned out, heaven was not quite as easily reached as I had assumed. The problem was not biological, but the artifice of human ingenuity. As I embraced my wife, I noticed something odd in the vicinity of her waist. Not having hugged a women in a negligee before, I assumed it had something to do with the garment. But the assumption didn't compute. Why in the world would they place coarse, rough material inside a negligee?

Upon further inspection, I discovered that the material had a familiar feel to it. *What's this?* I thought to myself, not wanting to voice my ignorance or let on that I was once again losing control. Before long it dawned on me that I was not touching a negligee at all, but an undergarment of some kind. And that the garment was not the least bit soft or silky.

Finally, I could stand the suspense no longer. And I allowed my eyes to look at what only my fingers had thus far envisioned. To my surprise—and the utter glee of my wife—I discovered, ensconced around her hips, a very tight pair of white cut-off jeans.

At first I was taken aback by this revelation. Not only was it unexpected but it quite dramatically changed the mood of the moment. Judy was having such an uproariously good time about the thing, however, that I eventually managed to regain my sense of humor and enter into the merriment of the occasion.

In due time, I took the jeans as not only a joke but a bit of a challenge, and I was fast about the business of removing them (not an easy task, I might add). But beneath the jeans was neither silk nor satin, but another pair of pants! Followed by another. And another. Between the layers of material and the convulsing hysterics of my wife, I would estimate that it took a good thirty minutes before I reached ... well, what other husbands reach in a good deal less time than that.

In the name of decency, you would expect this story to end at this point, wouldn't you? But it doesn't. It turns out that not only had my lovely bride wrapped herself in protective clothing, but she had also managed to get into my suitcase the night before the wedding and sew shut the flies of all my underwear and pajamas. But if you think I'm going to tell you how I discovered that, you're crazy.

Love

The story of our honeymoon is an intimate one. I've told it to you not only to let you know the burden that I bear (just kidding, Judy), but to impress upon you the joy with which I entered into marriage.

I had a wife that I loved deeply and without qualification. My father—a farmer not inclined to unleash many words of praise—took me aside on our wedding day and said, "Son, Judy's the best thing you've ever done." He said it with a smile, but I knew he was serious. And I knew he was right as well. There was no one I cared for more than Judy. And I loved her with a passion that was profound and all consuming.

And yet, within a year and a half of our marriage, I was bored. Not with Judy. Not with our relationship. But with that which was supposed to be at the core of my passion. The thing that guys talk about endlessly in the locker room was suddenly not worth talking about. The item that sells everything from toothpaste to automobiles hardly moved me at all. I would come home in the middle of the afternoon and, rather than sweep my wife off her feet, which is what any red-blooded American male would have done with glee—I would peel a banana instead.

This odd behavior pattern was no doubt encouraged by my schedule. I was a graduate student at the time and very much absorbed in my own world of studies and academic accomplishment. I had not applied myself as an undergraduate and consequently had never known the exhilaration of serious study. Graduate school changed all that. I buckled down, was rewarded with good grades, and felt the delight of academic success. As a result, the academic world became intoxicating. And like all drugs, this one was purchased at a price.

Everything came to a head, however, around the end of my second year in graduate school, the time I was scheduled to take my comprehensive exams. These exams last sixteen hours and are spread out over two days. The process of preparing for and taking them is akin to going on an all-day eating binge and then throwing up at a designated place and time. Except that, in this case, the contents have to look as good coming up as they did going down. Needless to say, they are the occasion for a good deal of stress.

Judy, being a tidy person by nature and not wanting to stick around for the purge, decided to get out of the house. Actually, what happened was that she finished the term early (she too was in graduate school) and was offered summer-school employment in another town. We desperately needed the money and so agreed that she would take the job, even though it meant that we would have to be separated for a couple of weeks.

The time apart was both good and bad for me. It was good in that it allowed me to give full attention to my studies. Since I would no doubt have done that anyway, what it really did was allow me not to feel guilty about ignoring my wife. It was bad, however, in that I missed

Judy terribly. Without her not only the house was empty, but there was a vacancy in my heart as well.

What this means is that, as the two-week separation was coming to a close, I was absolutely shot. I had not slept well. I had consumed every ounce of cholesterol within a twenty-mile radius of our apartment. And I had done poorly on my exams. Or so I thought. It turns out that I had passed three of my four area exams with honors, but the faculty kept that bit of encouragement hidden from me until they were able to put me through the wringer with a follow-up oral exam.

I was so strung out that by the time I heard I had passed the comps, it hardly phased me. All I wanted to do was get out of town, find Judy, and vegetate for a spell. Unfortunately, I couldn't do that because on my first day of freedom, I was scheduled to be in a wedding in Northern California. Instead of hopping in my car and finding my wife, I had to take a five-hour drive so I could watch one of my best friends find his wife. It didn't seem fair.

But you'll remember that I have an unusual wife. And she was not about to let mere distance come between us and our reunion. So instead of waiting for me to return from the wedding, she made it up to the wedding herself.

And I will never forget the first moment I saw her. How she looked. How she looked at me. How her beauty seemed to fill the room and make everything around her seem pale in comparison. I know I'm starting to sound like something of a cross between a Rogers and Hammerstein musical and a Hallmark card, but it would take a creative artist to depict my feelings that night. Mere prose won't do.

And then, somewhere in the midst of my reverie, it struck me like a ton of bricks: This women is in love with me. Dumb, inconsiderate me. Me, the one who had been ignoring her for the last year or so. Me, the one who couldn't crack a smile until 11:59 in the morning. Me, the one who made about as much of a contribution to household maintenance as a termite. Me, the late blooming scholar who had forsaken his first love for a book.

What happened at the wedding, I don't know, because the next thing I remember, we were back in each others arms, in some seedy motel room in the suburbs of San Jose. But the environment didn't matter. Not a bit. Only the person did. And I loved Judy that night in a way I had never loved her before. Fully. Without calculation. And without any thought of what was in it for me.

And that made all the difference. Because for the first time in my life, I gave myself to someone else for the purpose of giving love rather than taking it. For the first time, I didn't care how I felt, but only how she felt. For the first time, I wasn't in pursuit of my pleasure, my only consideration was the joy that I could bring to the one I loved. For the first time in my life, I made love like a servant rather than one being served.

There are points in your life that seem to somehow hang suspended in time and space. That transcend the restrictions of finitude and allow you to escape the inertia of your own biography. Not for long perhaps, but just long enough to enable you to turn your life around. It happened on the day I dropped to my knees and accepted Jesus as my Savior. It happened on the morning that I walked along the roads of my father's farm and implored the Lord to direct my career. And it happened that night with Judy in that seedy motel room in San Jose, California.

And it was just as important. For I learned something as fundamentally biblical, as deeply spiritual, as anything I had ever learned before or since. Love, I finally discovered, is for the giving, not for the taking. And the pleasure that comes in love, does not come to those who are served, but to those who do the serving.

I wish I had known that on our wedding day, but I did not. Instead, I had been sold a bill of goods about sex, and I believed it. Indeed, I thought my beliefs were quite Christian. I knew that sex outside of marriage was wrong. I knew that sex was the ultimate act of union between a husband and wife and was therefore to be confined to the state of marriage. As a result, I assumed that the only Christian issue related to sex was when it was done. Not why. As long as sex is performed by a husband and wife, I assumed, then it will be everything our society says it will be. Fabulous. Exciting. Totally fulfilling. A never-ending orgy of pleasure and satisfaction.

But it isn't. And we consume one of our world's grandest lies when we believe otherwise. Indeed, sex-as-sex is a rather meaningless activity—able to bring a flurry of excitement for a moment, perhaps, but hardly worth devoting your life to. Or interrupting your studies over.

Unless . . . unless it is a vehicle for something more. Unless it is the expression of a desire, born not of self-satisfaction, but the satisfaction of another. Unless it is rooted—not in the mere fact that you love someone else, for love too can be only a means to self-gratification—but in a love consumed by the good of another. Dead to self. And lost in the desire for another's pleasure. Unless, that is, it is Christ, nailed to a cross, losing his life for us.

It will come as no surprise to those who know about love, that I had a wonderful time that night in San Jose. And though it is dangerous to do so, I could describe that night in precisely society's terms. It was fabulous. Exciting. Totally fulfilling. A never-ending orgy of satisfaction and pleasure. Moreover, on that night, Judy and I began what has turned out to be a joyful pilgrimage of learning to love one another. And I cannot tell a lie, it has been magnificent.

But—and this is one of those radically important "buts"—it was these things by default, not design. San Jose was not intended for my pleasure, it was intended for hers. It was not meant to bring me joy, but in fact it did anyway.

And that is the wonder of it all, as well as the danger. In giving love, we find it. But in taking love, we lose it. Even those of us who find love in the right way are tempted to forget the equation. Because those things that we find, we also want to keep. And yet love is not for keeping, it is for letting go. It is letting go of the pride that desires conquest. It is letting go of the pleasure that demands gratification. It is letting go of the control that requires manipulation.

Most of all, in our world, it is letting go of the self that seeks its own satisfaction. And oh what a difficult letting go that is! For in dismissing our self, we are letting go of our god—which may help to explain why true love is so difficult to find in the modern world.

A postscript needs to be added to this story. Our turning point in San Jose occurred on June 12, 1971. I remember that date for two reasons. First, because it is the anniversary of my good friend's wedding. And second, because it comes nine months before March 11, 1972, which is the birthday of our first child, Heather. Yep, you guessed it. Joy is not the only unintended consequence of giving your love to another!

Thanks be to God for his manifold blessings.

5

LIFE AS A
DECISION MAKER

Pragmatism

Eventually, college ends. At least that's what parents assume when they send their kids off to those hallowed halls. The idea is that you spend four or five years in college, receive a diploma, secure a job, and get on with life. It is not a great model, in my opinion—I'd just as soon the order were reversed—but it is the one we have. Most of us, anyway.

Some people manage to stay at college in perpetuity, however, and I happen to be one of them. That's not entirely my fault. During my senior year, I contemplated three careers, all of which would have rescued me from academia sooner or later.

First, there was law school, about which I knew absolutely nothing except that it sounded important and Perry Mason went there. So I stumbled through the LSAT exams, for which I had no preparation, and applied to Harvard Law (why start at the bottom?). It took Harvard at least twenty-four hours to reject me, and of course they were full of "regrets" about the whole thing.

My second option was to return home and go into farming with my dad. My father wasn't aware of this option, but I did consider it. From day one, Dad had told me that farming was risky business and that I'd be better off getting a good education and a stable occupation. I believed him but not for his reasons. My father was reasonably successful at his craft and—having no personal encounter with the anguish of risk taking—I assumed the income from farming was worth the risk. The problem with farming, from my perspective, was the nature of the beast: long hours and frequent solitude. I had encountered those things every summer during my youth, and I wasn't sure I could endure them full time. Nevertheless, I liked the thought of working with my dad.

There is irony in all of this because, years later, after I had become firmly ensconced in my first professorate, my father one day confessed to me that, deep down, he "kind of hoped" I would return to the farm. Not because he wanted me to go into farming—I don't think he even wanted to be a farmer himself—but because he would have enjoyed working with me. The greatest irony is that today, twenty years after I made the decision not to go into farming because of long hours and solitude, I get up at 5:30 every morning so I can write and keep ahead of my students. Don't tell me God doesn't have a sense of humor.

The third career option was to stay put and become a probation officer in Santa Barbara. This may not sound exciting compared to Harvard Law and farming, but you need to understand the whole picture. The key phrase in the above sentence, you see, is not "career" or "probation officer." It is "Santa Barbara." The college I attended was nestled in the hills of that lovely city. And since Judy and I were married before my senior year, we had the good fortune of spending our first year of marriage in one of the most beautiful settings west of New England. And we loved it. I even bought a small motorcycle so we could meander through the hills and along the back roads, exploring the aesthetic riches of the area, which were legion, as you might expect. And as a consequence, we didn't want to leave.

So when the probation office announced in the local newspaper that they had a couple of openings and would be giving a qualifying exam on Saturday, I signed up. Why not do something constructive for society? Why not help ex-cons get back on their feet? Why not serve my fellow man, using the gifts God had given me and the social sensitivities my education had provided? Why not stay in Santa Barbara?

It is wonderful to serve the Lord, I thought to myself as I marched into the room where the qualifying exam was being given, sat down, and began taking the test. My buoyancy must have spilled over onto the exam because I moved through it like a hot knife on butter. *Piece of cake,* I thought to myself a few hours later, as I finished the last question. And my analysis proved correct. Within a few days, I learned that I had scored well on the exam. All I had to do now was sit back and wait for the probation office to call.

And so I waited. And waited. And waited. Eventually, I could stand the suspense no longer and called the probation office about my status. Some very bored secretary put me through to an even more lethargic administrator who informed me that I was number sixty-two on the waiting list and that my number would come up . . . oh, in about forty-five years. Maybe a little less. I tried to take heart from his last comment. "Maybe a little less," I told Judy hopefully. But even forty years seemed a long time to wait for a job, regardless of its location. I let out a deep sigh. Apparently a lot of people wanted to serve the Lord in Santa Barbara.

We would have to leave. That was the bottom line. We also had to figure out where to go and to some that would have been the more perplexing matter. But not to me. The salient fact was that we were going to have to move on. Away from the hills. Away from our friends. Away from our first apartment. Away from the environment that had nourished our love in the first place, and without which one wondered if love—and even life—could survive.

The thought of having to move played a major role in our next decision. Contemplating the loss of Santa Barbara, I couldn't bear the idea of returning to the farm. The contrast was just too great. From moist to dry. From green to brown. From hills to a valley. From trees to plants. From coastline to power lines. From ocean waves to waves of grain. It was just too much. "How you gonna keep them down on the farm, after they've seen Paree?" was not the problem. The farm had a lot of appeal. The problem was Santa Barbara. And the ache God gave me for green, salty places.

There were other considerations as well. Judy had one more year of college so we needed to be near a good school. And I had a growing interest in sociology, though I wasn't sure I wanted to trust my career to it. The answer, we decided, was a university, not too far from the ocean, that would allow Judy to finish her education, give me a chance to dabble in sociology at the graduate school level, and provide both of us with some degree of aesthetic satisfaction.

We didn't find it. Instead, we wound up at a university located in the suburbs of Southern California, nearly an hour from the ocean, ringed with apartments and three-bedroom homes that looked just alike, peopled with 20,000 students who looked just alike, studded with buildings that looked just alike, and decorated by a total of one-and-a-half trees.

To make matters worse, we decided we ought to live relatively near campus, so we secured an apartment even more barren than the university. It didn't have any trees at all and, while it did have a balcony, it overlooked a freeway on-ramp. Consequently, not only was the view questionable, but we were regularly entertained by trucks and motorcycles hitting mach 4 by the time they entered the freeway. Lying in bed, I tried to pretend the waves of engine noises were really the pounding of the surf. But there was nothing I could do with a Mack truck. Even a whale with a stomachache would be ashamed to make such sounds.

The question is how did we manage to go from Santa Barbara to this? After all, we had a hard time leaving Santa Barbara for aesthetic reasons. So why did we choose Blah City?

The answer is that we made good head decisions, but lost our hearts in the process. The university had a decent program in sociology (my concern), an excellent reputation in elementary education (Judy's interest), and kept us within a few hours' drive of friends and family. For all these reasons, it seemed like a good choice. We knew it was ugly, but we convinced ourselves that we could survive the uglies for a year or two. Besides, how important is a view anyway? Our love affair with Santa Barbara was really a bit silly, wasn't it? What practical value is there to blue sky and a little greenery here and there?

Probably none. But its absence gave rise to one of the bleakest, most dismal years of our lives. On the surface, things were fine. We ate three meals a day. Attended all our classes. Kept the house clean. Buckled down to our studies and received good marks. In other words, nothing was obviously wrong. Our health was good. We kept up a normal schedule. Stayed in close contact with family and friends. We lived a normal life.

Nevertheless, something was wrong. Dreadfully wrong. We didn't fully understand it at the time. And I don't ever remember sitting down and saying, "The uglies are getting us down." Life as a couple was too new for us to know our limitations. What we knew, however, was that something had changed. There was an emptiness in our lives that was almost indescribable. A palor too bleak to comprehend. And it wasn't until we had some distance from it—a year or so later—that we figured out the problem.

What struck us initially was how few happy memories we had there. Good friends had visited us. We had celebrated birthdays and at least one anniversary. In short, we had many experiences that should have been memorable. But they were not. It was almost as if the year was covered with a drab veneer that hid the highlights and exposed the flaws. And sitting here today, twenty years later, I can't recall one significant event that occurred in that apartment. All I remember are shades of pale. And Mack trucks.

How important is setting anyway? Or how important should it be? Those are not easy questions to answer. On the one hand, many Christians have the gnawing suspicion that they ought to be above such things, that their need for hills and greenery and ocean beauty is evidence of weakness. If we were really in control, we tell ourselves, we would set those concerns aside and get on with life. "Follow the Lord wherever he may lead," this voice tells us, "and let the setting take care of itself."

Following the Lord is good advice, of course. And that's all I want to do. But it's this business of treating the setting as if it is of no consequence that bothers me! That's what we did when we enrolled in Blah University, remember? That's the voice that told us to be practical, focus on your objectives, and make the right decision. But the decision we made on that basis turned out to be a poor one. It did not strengthen our resolve. It did nothing for our marriage. It turned study into a joyless exercise. It made serving our neighbor a near impossibility, not to mention loving him. And it cast a pall over our lives that can only be described as a form of spiritual oppression.

It was not a decision that was irredeemable, of course. For the Christian, there is no such thing. And because of that year, I came to learn a great deal about myself, the way God had created me, and the limits of practical decision making.

But the most important thing I learned is that God made us creatures for whom setting is important. Our environment is significant. Not only because we need it for survival, but we need it for spiritual refreshment as well. We are creatures designed to appreciate the work of a Creator. Some of us find our appreciation in the desert. Others on an expanse of prairie. And still others in the hills by a bay. God has given us a great deal of variety to choose from. But about the act of appreciation, we have no choice. We do it. Or we are less than the people God created us to be in the first place.

And as hard as it may be for a practical person like me to admit, we are fools if we fail to bring that reality into our decision making. Fools and shortcomers.

Foolishness

I was sitting in Ugly Building #13 when the rescue commenced. There were nine of us in the class plus Dr. Chevy, erstwhile human being and now professor of sociological theory. He spent the first half hour grinning and handing out reading assignments, taking great glee in the general incomprehensibility of the assigned material. As he well knew, his reputation preceded him. He did not give A's and his only delight was in inflicting pain on graduate students.

After he was convinced that he had sufficiently terrified everyone in the room, he asked each student to talk a little bit about themselves: where they had done their undergraduate work; what their preparation in sociology was like; how much social theory they had under their belts; that sort of thing. Make no mistake, he didn't do this to ease the tension. Quite the reverse. The plan was first to convince us how difficult the course was going to be, after which we would have to contemplate how ill prepared we were for such an encounter. And he relished every minute of it.

The inquisition proceeded in an orderly fashion.

The first few students were graduates of Blah University and thus already known to Dr. Chevy. They shared a few inside jokes, and it was obvious that one of them was in a class by himself. Relaxed and confident, he bantered with the professor as an equal. Later I learned that he had received the highest grade in Dr. Chevy's senior seminar the prior year, and that he was an A-1 bona fide teacher's pet.

"So, what have we here," Dr. Chevy droned out condescendingly. "Mr. Gade, is it?"

"Uh . . . no," I said, starting the conversation out with my favorite word, "Dr. Chevy. It's, uh, 'Gaa-dee.'"

"Gaa-dee?" he said in almost mocking tones. "That's an odd pronunciation. What is it, Lithuanian or something?" This was said in a pejorative tone and A-1 feigned a slight smirk. As I tried to think up a response, I wondered what the Lithuanian people had done to earn his ire.

"Uh, no. It's German actually. An Americanized version of the German name, Goethe." That was true in all probability, but I said it with more authority than it deserved. Someone in the family had researched the name and, while it is undoubtedly German, "Goethe" is only a best guess regarding its origin. But I needed ammunition. And being related to the smartest man in German history seemed a good way to begin loading up.

"Oh," he said, almost crestfallen. "Well, why don't you tell us a little bit about your background and preparation for this course."

"Uh . . . okay. I, uh, graduated from a small liberal arts college in Santa Barbara. . . ." And I went on to explain that my primary interests were in sociology and history, with a particular focus in secularization, but I could tell that he had heard nothing beyond the first sentence. Indeed, the minute I said "small," his pupils hit maximum dilation. And by the time I finished my comments, he looked like a dog preparing to devour a T-bone steak.

"Sssssmall?" he hissed. "How ssssmall is it?"

"Under a thousand students," I responded, overstating the case but not falling into a lie.

"And how much social theory have you been exposed to at this ... er ... ssssmall college?"

"I, uh, actually had two quarters of theory, plus an independent study on ..." And off I went again, this time talking about a research project, and surprising myself with the number of details I remembered. Indeed, I felt quite good about my response because I knew that most undergraduates in sociology at Blah University only took a single semester of social theory. But again, I could tell that Professor Chevy was not very interested in the details.

"Tell me," he broke in before I had a chance to complete my thought. "Do you reeeeally think you're adequately prepared for this course? We don't start at the beginning, you know. We're starting with Marcuse and going on from there. There will be no time for clarification questions on Durkheim, Weber, and Marx. I'm assuming you've read that stuff and have them down pat. This isn't college anymore."

He wasn't talking only to me. He was using me to make a point to the whole class. Many of my classmates were, like me, first-year graduate students, and he wanted us to know the difficulties that lay ahead. More than anything, he wanted us to understand that he was a tough taskmaster who delighted in thinning out the ranks. And the thinning process was beginning right now.

I didn't realize all of this at the time, of course. All I knew was that he was not listening to me. That he was using me for target practice. And that I was on the verge of looking like a fool in front of my peers. Two emotions tangled together immediately. First, fear that my graduate career was fast coming to a halt. And second, anger, because I felt unfairly victimized by his potshots.

I sat there without saying a word, primarily because I didn't know what to say, but also because fear had swollen my tongue to twice its normal size. I was stuck. The eyes of my prof—like those in the rest of the room— were also stuck. On me. And I made every effort to give them a satisfactory answer. But try as I might, I couldn't get the equipment in gear.

As the seconds of silence continued to tick away, I noticed that something was beginning to happen. Professor Cool was becoming less so, and his countenance was increasingly looking perplexed. Upon completing his "are you prepared" harangue, he was absolutely in control. But with each moment of silence, he seemed to be loosing his composure. And so, not being able to say anything anyway, and remembering the effectiveness of my father's silent treatment, I decided to milk the hush for all it was worth.

I don't know how long we sat there—eighteen eyes looking at me for a response, and me acting as if one wasn't necessary. Finally, however, I could bear the suspense no longer. I straightened up in my chair. Crossed my legs to keep my knees from knocking. Screwed up my courage. Looked Dr. Chevy in the eyes. And with all the nonchalance I could muster, simply said, "I can handle it." It was not the most elegant self-defense in the world, but it was all I could manage.

And it seemed to work. Dr. Chevy nervously looked down at his class roster and began picking on someone else. And I began to believe that an "A" from Chevy was not as formidable a task as my classmates seemed to assume.

Regardless of my newfound confidence, you will understand why, when class finally ended, I was planning to make a beeline straight for the bathroom. Before I got halfway out of my chair, however, I was accosted by another student, who sat down in the chair beside me and stuck out his hand.

"Hi. I'm Patrick Christiansen." He paused. And the way he did it made me wonder if he expected a round of applause. "That was nice," he continued with a grin the size of California, while flipping his head over in the direction of Dr. Chevy, who was now deeply involved in a conversation with Barry Brown Nose. "Very, very nice."

"Uh, well, thanks," I said. "The guy's kind of intimidating, you know."

"Oh, gosh, don't I know it!" he laughed. "I could tell you stories. . . ." He paused again, but this time for a thought, not an applause. And when he put his mouth back in gear, he said something that nearly knocked me off my chair. "Tell me, Stan—it is Stan, isn't it?—tell me, Stan [another pause] . . . are you a Christian?"

I was floored. Here I was in the ugliest place in the world, sitting with people who didn't believe in each other, much less God, trying to blend in with the scenery, and suddenly Sociable Swede asks me, "Are you a Christian?" I couldn't believe it. First, the inquisitor picks on me for coming from a "ssssmall college." And now I'm being accused of being a Christian. What was I doing wrong anyway?

"Well, uh . . . ," I stammered, "I grew up in a, uh . . . well, I attended a, uh. . . ."

I looked around the room to see if anyone else was watching. Only a few students remained, and they were desperately trying to impress Herr Professor. I decided to confess.

"Well, yes, I am a Christian," I whispered. "But how in the world did you know that? I mean," lowering my voice even still, "why do you ask?"

The smile continued at full strength and I half suspected he would reach for the sky and begin singing, "Praise the Lord! Oh my soul! And all that is within me praise his hooooooooly name." Which of course would have ended my academic career right there and been a fitting conclusion to my day, if not my life.

But he did not. Instead, he leaned back like a therapist who had finally figured out his client, and said, "Oh, I don't know. I just suspected you might be. The way you handled yourself in class, I guess. But I'm really not sure. It just hit me that you might be."

He took a pleased pause this time, and then began self-disclosing. "I'm a second-year graduate student and hoping to finish my Master's degree this spring. I work part time at the Hollywood Awfullygood Church, sort of as a youth pastor, but I assist the pastor in other ways as well. You may have heard of it. It's right downtown Hollywood. Ronald Reagan is a member, though he rarely attends. Anyway, the church owns a complex of four apartments behind the sanctuary, and so my wife—Mandy—and I live there. It's a ways from campus, but a great deal for us. . . ."

He proceeded to tell me a bit about his background, periodically asking me questions for comparative purposes. And as we talked for the next hour or so—alone now in the classroom—two things struck me about my new acquaintance.

First, I liked him. He was an extremely friendly fellow and amazingly open to boot. The man had no guile. He said what he thought, regardless of the consequences. This got him into trouble sometimes—when he revealed more than he should have—but it endeared him to me. Partly, I suppose, because I'm not that way. And partly because I wish I were.

Secondly—and this needs to be said more delicately because it could be misunderstood, especially in today's atmosphere—Patrick was a liberal. Not politically or socially necessarily, but theologically. He grew up in a mainline Protestant church and continued to be affiliated with mainline churches. Of course, there is a lot of variety in those churches today, and they have members who run the gamut theologically. But in the late sixties, liberalism was very "in" in many mainline denominations, especially among the clergy. And while Patrick wasn't all that interested in theology—in fact, he tended to avoid theological disputes if at all possible—the little he had definitely came from the liberal camp.

This fact put Patrick at odds with me since I was both theologically conservative and theologically inclined. In other words, I was an evangelical who argued a lot. Patrick was not and didn't much care. The surprising thing was how little this seemed to affect our friendship. There are a number of reasons for this, I think, not the least of which was that Patrick was a congenial soul who could have gotten along with Genghis Khan. But more importantly, Patrick acted more like an evangelical than I did.

Our first meeting is a case in point. Who is it that comes up and asks, on first acquaintance, "Are you a Christian?" Harvey Cox? Bishop Pike? Hardly. They might solicit your attendance at a revolution or a séance, but they would hardly request your status relative to the kingdom. But Patrick did, in no equivocal terms. Indeed, he was so forthright about it at our first meeting that I was afraid he might go songspirational on me. For Patrick, it was a natural question which flowed from his faith. He wouldn't get bent out of shape if the answer was, "No." But on the other hand, he didn't get that answer very often. He had a nose for Christ followers.

But there was a certain foolishness about Patrick, that no doubt frustrated his family and friends at times— we've all got stories to tell and his wife could write a book—but nevertheless struck me as deeply spiritual and right. For example, after high school Patrick went to one of the finest universities in the Midwest. During the middle of his college career, however, he and a couple friends who had formed a folk group decided to quit college, move to L.A., and make a career out of singing. Which they did. In fact, they became fairly successful at it, touring with one of Hollywood's legends, singing background music for two Disney movies, and performing on their own.

But after five or six years with the group, Patrick decided to go back to college. And this appeared even more foolish than the decision to leave college in the first place. The group was successful. They were cutting records. They were, it seemed, on the edge of making it big. This was not the time to throw in the towel. This was the time to reach for the stars. To go for the gold.

But foolishly Patrick said, "No." Instead of going for the gold, he enrolled in Blah University and took a job as youth pastor at a local church. What that meant, of course, is that he went from being the center of attention to being one of 20,000 students in Ugly Building #13. And even worse, he went from potential stardom to a chump organizing church basketball games for kids who couldn't care less. It was a move that defied logic. As stupid an idea as any person ever came up with.

And Patrick felt its pain. Not at church, for he seemed to find absolute delight in turning careless kids into caring young people. But school was another matter. There, students seven years his junior were already graduating from college and moving on to successful careers. More than once he told me that he felt like a square peg in a round hole. His peers were not the students around him, after all, but doctors and lawyers who were already well along in their practices. His peers were successes—as he had been, not aspiring students.

And sometimes he wondered if he was the craziest guy on earth.

But not usually. Usually, it was full steam ahead, without knowing exactly where he was going. He picked his major because it interested him, not because it would lead to any career. He went fishing on weekends, even though he had a test on Monday, because the fish were there. He spent a year studying abroad because Sweden was there. And now he was pursuing a Master's degree in sociology at Blah University because it was there. One foolish decision after another.

And yet, and yet . . . today, some twenty years later, Dr. Patrick Christiansen is one of the nation's foremost psychotherapists, a leading authority on the treatment of alcohol and drug abuse, helping people who are down in the pit to crawl out. But I shouldn't say, "And yet." Because Patrick is still doing what he always did. Still helping careless kids care. Still going fishing on weekends and sometimes going to Sweden as well. Still asking strangers if they're Christians. Still pursuing one foolish idea after another, just because it seems right. Because making the most out of what God has given is more important than making sense.

That was something I didn't understand when we moved to Blah City. Making sense was all that mattered, I thought. And as a result, we ended up making ourselves miserable. And doing a pretty good job of wasting away part of our lives as well.

But foolish Patrick was not about to let that happen. Not once he got to know us, anyway, and that didn't take long. Within a month I discovered that he couldn't figure out the meaning of a null hypothesis, and he learned I that couldn't resist losing a game of tennis. That seemed to be enough to draw us together periodically. Eventually, I got him through his statistics comprehensive. He got me back in shape. And Patrick, Mandy, Judy, and Stan became good friends.

I can't remember how it came about but, in due time, Patrick picked up on our dissatisfaction with the apartment. I honestly don't remember complaining about it. You'll remember that I thought our situation was the price we had to pay for being practical. And practical people don't complain. But Patrick was already a therapist at heart and I'm sure he detected some degree of dissatisfaction on our part. No doubt, the fact that I turned green every time I crossed the threshold of our apartment was a clue.

Anyway, one day Patrick stormed into our apartment. "Have I got news for you," he announced with all the finesse of a used-car dealer. "The old lady in our front apartment died last night!"

Now, I have known elderly Christians so excited about heaven that they look forward to death. And I have been to funerals that are as much a celebration of a loved one's homegoing, as they are a mourning of the loved one's passing. But I can't recall anyone ever being quite so happy about anyone's death as Patrick.

"Well, indeed, this is good news, Patrick," I chimed in heartily. "If we're really lucky, the young couple living upstairs will kick off tonight." Judy chuckled in the next room but Patrick never missed a beat.

"She was a dear soul but not very sociable. Regular churchgoer, though, and a good neighbor. I think she was dead for a few days before they discovered her body. Her daughter couldn't reach her by phone, so dropped by late last night to see what was the matter. There she was, lying in her bed, peaceful as can be—but a bit ripe."

"Again, Patrick, let me tell you how pleased I am to hear this. And to think: You drove twenty miles through L.A. traffic just to deliver the news. With friends like you—"

"Stan, you innocent! Don't you get it? Her apartment is now vacant. The church will be looking for a new tenant. It will be on the market next week at 95 dollars per month—95 dollars! Do you know how many apartments there are in Hollywood for 95 dollars per month?"

I couldn't imagine. We were paying 145 dollars for our apartment in Blah City. And while Patrick's apartment wasn't in the Hollywood Hills, it was on the edge, with forty-foot palm trees lining the street and semi-green hills only two blocks away. Suffice it to say, it was a lush paradise compared to where we were living. Best of all, it was within the L.A. basin, which meant it was vulnerable to the ocean breezes and ten to fifteen degrees cooler than Blah City. True, it was Hollywood, which meant that you were vulnerable to a lot more than ocean breezes. But, I knew we would love it.

"Patrick," I said with a sigh, "the price is wonderful. But if we don't stay here for a year, we'll lose a month's rent. That means we're stuck with this apartment for at least two more months. We can't move now. Besides, your place is nearly thirty minutes from the university. We'd spend at least an hour every day on the road. That hardly seems practical to me."

Patrick scrunched up his nose. Practical was not what he had in mind when he made his offer. In fact, practical was not in his vocabulary. He proceeded as if my words had no meaning.

"Look, you guys, I can get you in. But you'll need to act now. Once we place it on the open market, I can't hold it for you. Besides, it's going to go quickly...." He paused to study our sterile apartment for a few moments, coming to rest on the sliding glass door, overlooking the balcony, overlooking the freeway on-ramp, overlooking endless miles of pale. "I make the drive to the university every day, you know. It's no big deal. What is a big deal is coming back home in the evening, going over the

Hollywood Hills, feeling the air turn fifteen degrees cooler, and knowing you're home."

He could have shoved an ice pick under my finger nails and given me less pain. And that made the decision all the more difficult. Lurking in the attraction of his offer lay much that I had deemed "wrong" in the past. It was an appeal to the heart, and that alone made it suspect. We had to decide quickly, and I had been schooled on the philosophy that "any offer that can't wait is an offer worth waiting on." It was going to mean throwing 145 dollars down the drain, and we were scraping the bottom of the barrel as it was. And it wasn't necessary. We had a decent apartment. We didn't need to move. We didn't need a thing. It was all wrong.

"It's all right." Patrick paused. "It's all right with me if you wait until Monday to make your decision. We have at least that much time. But I do ask that you come down and look it over—once we get the smell out of the room. Just kidding. You'll love it. I know it."

"One more thing," Patrick continued as he walked toward the door. "We live there, remember? Patrick and Mandy? We'd love to have you guys for neighbors. Would you consider moving there for us?"

You bet, Patrick. Anytime. Anytime at all.

And so we spent the next year living in Hollywood. In three months, we saved enough on rent to make up for the loss at On-Ramp Heights, walked enough hills to overcome the atrophy in our muscles, drank in enough fresh air and greenery to replenish our souls, and heard enough of Patrick's dreams to say, "Come on Patrick, cut the baloney. Get down to earth. Be practical. Get real."

*And thanks be to God, he didn't pay
any attention to us whatsoever.*

6

LIFE AT
BIRTH

Expectations

I don't know how other hopeful fathers view childbirth, but I know that I had definite expectations about it. For one thing, I knew that the birth of our first child would be a thrilling moment in our lives. After all, we had been looking forward to it for ... oh, seven or eight days now, and the excitement was starting to get unbearable.

Secondly, I was pretty certain that childbirth was a somewhat holy event, marked by hushed tones, meaningful sighs, and deep emotional bonds. This expectation was encouraged by other men who were already fathers—especially by those who had actually witnessed the birth itself, as I planned to do. When they talked about it, their voices cracked, their lips began to quiver, and there was the sense that they had gone through a deeply spiritual experience.

Finally, I knew it was going to be an important time in my life. And even more than that, I would be an important part of it. After all, it was my child who was being born. I was one of the two major players in this event. It only seemed natural that my role would be pivotal and that, from the experience, I would garner a good deal of respect, status, and self-esteem.

So it was with a good deal of excitement that Judy and I awaited the birth of our first child. That had not always been the case, by the way. In spite of the magnificent event that had produced this baby (remember the seedy motel in San Jose?), news of the pregnancy was not met with thunderous applause. The problem, once again, was school.

I was still in it, for one thing—having graduated from Blah with a Master's degree and moved back east to begin work on a Ph.D.—and that had serious financial implications. But more importantly, Judy had finally graduated and was about to embark on a marvelous career as a kindergarten teacher. Marvelous, first, because she was a natural in the classroom. But marvelous too because we desperately needed her income. At first blush, therefore, the pregnancy seemed to cast doubt both upon my graduate career and her earning potential. About the only thing it demonstrated was the fecundity of true love.

The Lord, however, having blessed the night in San Jose in the first place, had no intention of letting us wallow in despair for long. He quickly arranged for a part-time teaching job for me, a grandmother who was willing to fly halfway across the country to care for the newborn, and a generous stipend from the university. More amazing still, when the cost of medical care finally reared its ugly head, he hooked us into a university medical plan that covered all expenses for 400 dollars. Even in 1972, that was a phenomenal deal.

One other interesting Sovereign feat. A few weeks before Judy actually delivered, the doctors decided to induce labor since the baby was late. Well, Heather wasn't ready to come yet, so she didn't (a prophetic act if ever there was one). It turns out, however, that inducing

labor was about the only procedure not covered by the
university medical plan, which meant we had to come
up with an additional 100 dollars to pay for an unpro-
ductive induction. Well, wouldn't you know it, the Lord
had allowed a thief to break into our Volkswagen van and
steal our radio, for which the insurance company paid us
exactly $100. The theology of that one still baffles me.
But the practical consequences were much appreciated.
Who can hear the radio in a VW van anyway?

By the time the baby was *really* ready, we were too.
We had created a cozy little room for her in the back of
the apartment. Decorated it blue, because she was going
to be a boy ("strong heartbeat," the doctor said, "it'll be a
boy"). Taken natural childbirth classes with all the other
trendy couples who ate granola and suffered through the
sixties. And of course, I had conjured up all those
expectations about the thrill, holiness, and importance of
childbirth. We were ready.

My first indication that something was wrong came
at about 2:00 A.M. on March 11. It consisted of water all
over our double bed. That is an absolute no-no in our
house. Water is for bathrooms, kitchens, and lawns, but
definitely not for bedrooms. My wife was appalled by
this indiscretion, and so immediately did two things.
First, she ripped the sheets off the bed (as I rolled gently
onto the bedroom floor) and threw them in the washing
machine. And second, she took a shower.

Now, of course, as I sat there on the floor in my
underwear at 2:00 in the morning, the question that
immediately came to mind was, Why? Facile mind that I
have, I eventually remembered something about "the
waters breaking" at the onslaught of childbirth, and I
assumed that something like that had occurred moments
before in our bedroom. The real question was, why are
we washing the sheets? And why is The Pregnant One

taking a shower? Why, in fact, aren't we racing to the hospital to have our baby?

I had a great deal of time to ponder these questions, by the way, because my wife decided not only to take a shower, but also to shave her legs, condition her hair, polish her nails, and otherwise prepare her body for the Second Coming. "How can this be?" I kept asking myself. She is supposed to be crippled over with pain, begging me to take her to the hospital, and listening to me say soothing, manly things, like, "Everything's going to be all right, honey. I'll take care of everything." Instead, she was singing in the shower and I was in a stupor on the floor. Something was definitely wrong.

Eventually, I got off the floor and into a modestly respectful outfit. It wasn't long, though, before I too was in the house cleaning mode, whipping the vacuum cleaner out of the closet and pretending it was Saturday. This wasn't because I suddenly saw the wisdom of Judy's ways. ("Oh, of course. The house must be spick-and-span before the baby is born! What would she think, coming home to an unmade bed!") The problem was, the minute Judy got out of the shower, she immediately began barking out instructions:

"Make sure the living room is straightened out, would you please, Stan? And would you mind going over the carpets quickly with the vacuum cleaner, as well? You're a dear. You might want to check to see if the sheets are ready to be thrown into the dryer, while you're at it." And so on.

Now, I thought about debating her on these points. I knew I had logic on my side, in fact. After all, the doctor's instructions were quite explicit. "Get to the hospital right away if the water breaks." There was nothing there about rearranging the furniture or giving the carpet a good shampoo.

But I had a problem. Judy is a very determined

woman when it comes to how things ought to be done. She doesn't force them on me, but she doesn't let me stop her from getting them done either. If I would have said, "No, honey, I will not clean the house; we must get to the hospital immediately," she would have smiled pleasantly, grabbed the vacuum cleaner, and done it herself. I would have continued talking. And she would have continued working. And what she wanted doing would have gotten done anyway. It just would have taken a little longer, that's all.

So, if I wanted her to get to the hospital quickly, I had only one option and that was to do what she asked. Which I did. Which meant that, at the time other husbands are racing to the hospital in their cars, cooing soothing words of comfort in their wives' ears, I was pushing our vacuum cleaner up and down the hall, mumbling incoherently to myself, and beginning to wonder about my expectations concerning childbirth.

It would not be the last time.

When we finally arrived at the hospital (some two days later, it seemed), they were ready for us. Not that the hospital was as clean as our apartment, mind you, but it was pretty close. And of course the nurses were all very kind and appreciative ("Oh look, Madge, she had her hair done for the delivery; isn't that just about the cutest thing you've ever seen?"). They quickly ushered Judy into the labor room and told me that I could join her in a few minutes.

It wasn't long before I was sitting by Judy's side. And things were looking up, as far as I was concerned. My wife was finally in a hospital bed, for one thing, and that was a change for the better. But she was also starting to have serious contractions and that meant pain couldn't be far behind. Now I wasn't pleased about her pain, obviously; I'd had kidney stones so I knew something about the pain she was going to go through. But I also knew that I couldn't play my cooing, soothing role until she needed to be cooed and soothed. And I needed to be needed.

It was at this point that another problem emerged. I said earlier that water-in-the-bedroom is a no-no in our family. Well, it turns out, so is crying, not to mention screams and wails. Even whimpers are suspect. Tears of joy are fine, by the way, as are laughter and cries of merriment. We can be absolutely Italian where fun is concerned. But pain is quite another matter. When it arrives, we immediately become Swedish. A contortion of the eyebrow is about all that is allowed.

As the hours dragged on, therefore, Judy's eyebrows kept arching higher and higher, but not a single complaint issued from her lips. I could hear screams coming from the other labor rooms. The Lord's name seemed to be on everybody's mind. And I knew that husbands all over the hospital were saying, "That's all right, honey; I'm going to stay right by your side; breathe in deeply now—that's it, that's it, GOOOOOD!" But in our room, nothing. Not a creature was stirring, not even a spouse.

Now, none of this should suggest that Judy was quiet or melancholy during this time. Or the least bit uncommunicative. Quite the contrary, she wanted to talk. But she wanted to talk about me! She asked me questions about my classes. She wanted to know how my part-time teaching job was going, who was taking my place in the classroom that day, and how I was feeling about my dissertation research. "Not good," I lied, feeling about as useful as an appendix. And in minutes, I found myself babbling incessantly, complaining about all manner of things, and generally using the session for therapeutic purposes.

It was some place in the middle of my nineteenth complaint that the doctor came in, examined Judy, and proclaimed, "She's almost fully dilated; let's get her into the delivery room." He turned around and looked at me in disdain, "Are you the father?" he asked in disbelief. I nodded, still trying to finish my last complaint. "Then stop talking and get your butt down to the dressing room; she's about to deliver."

As they wheeled Judy down the hall, I sprinted in the other direction, trying to find the doctors' dressing room. Eventually, I found what I thought was the right door and walked in. When I entered the room, however, all I could see was a wall full of lockers and a young man with long curly hair taking a nap on a narrow wooden bench in the center of the room. I stood at the door for a few seconds and inspected the room; drab green walls, darker green lockers, and army-green floors. This can't be the right room, I thought to myself; this looks just like my own graduate student study room across campus.

My intrusion had apparently awakened the young man. "Can I help you with something?" he asked politely, as he wiped the sleep from his eyes and assumed a semi-upright position. His hair now dangled below his shoulder and I thought to myself, *Either he works for maintenance or he's a fellow graduate student in sociology.*

"Yeah," I quickly responded. "I'm supposed to prep for delivery; my wife is going to have a baby."

"Good," he said with a smile, "I'm supposed to deliver one in a few minutes. My name's John Farnsworth." He reached out to shake my hand and, after giving it a few pumps, pointed across the room. "The robes are over there; just grab one that looks the right size."

I fumbled around amongst the robes, but I couldn't take my eyes off my new friend. "John," I said very hesitantly, "are you, uh ... are you a physician?"

"Brand new," he responded with the same broad grin. "I'm an intern here at the hospital. This is my day to deliver babies. Interns get a chance to do a lot of different things," he continued. "It gives us the opportunity to be exposed to a variety of procedures. Something new every day. It's tiring, but I love it. That nap was the first rest I've had in twenty-four hours."

I didn't say anything so he continued. "Are you at the university?" he queried, still smiling and still trying to wake up.

"That's right," I said. "I'm a grad student in the sociology department; I teach a few courses as well."

"Sociology!" His eyes lit up. "Oh, I loved sociology when I was an undergraduate. In fact, I almost decided to major in it. But my heart was set on med school and I just couldn't work it in. I did manage to take quite a few soc courses, however. Do you know anything about C. Wright Mills?"

Now, I must tell you, it is not often that you find a physician who has read anything by C. Wright Mills. Or anything by any other sociologist for that matter. And of course, I should have been thrilled by this revelation— this bit of camaraderie. But in all honesty, I wasn't looking for a sociologically informed physician at that moment. Nor was I looking for youth. Long hair. Or friendship. In fact, I rather had in mind a man in his forties, graying around the temples, eyes bright from plenty of rest, face tanned from successful days on the golf course, and fingers trained from lots of experience. I wouldn't have even minded a tad of arrogance in a trade-off for expertise.

And then it hit me. I wanted that doctor who had told me to get my butt down to the dressing room. He was my idea of a real physician.

"Uh ... yea, a little," I said, responding to his question about Mills. "Uh, who was that doctor who was attending my wife back in the labor room?" I asked, impolitely cutting off his interest in my profession.

"Oh, that's James Stinson. He's the head resident around here. He's the one who is technically in charge of your wife's delivery. But don't worry about a thing. I'm the one who's actually going to perform the delivery," he said with a grin. "See you in the delivery room. Long live C. Wright Mills," he laughed, as he gave me the ubiquitous two-finger, V salute.

"Peace," I responded despairingly.

"Oh, by the way," he said almost as an afterthought. "That's a surgical mask you've got around your waist, not a jock strap. You'll want to put that over your mouth and nose. Ciao."

Deliveries

By the time I walked into the delivery room, I was shot. Most of my expectations had come to naught. The thrill of childbirth had been replaced by high anxiety and deep depression. The assumption that I was an important player in this event could only be considered true to the extent that Curly is an important character in the Three Stooges. Errol Flynn I was not. And my wife—my beautiful, lovely, wife—was under the care of the friendliest guy in town. Mr. Warmth. Mr. Sociology. Marcus Welby, Brand New.

My only hope was that the "holiness expectation" might somehow still come true. That I would walk into the delivery room and finally find the atmosphere I was looking for. A surgical cathedral. Men and women in beautiful robes, surrounding my wife in rapt attention, movements regulated by the liturgy of childbirth, while strains of Beethoven's Ninth could be faintly heard in the background. I too would be part of the picture again. A slight bow from the doctors would greet me as I breezed into the delivery room. An orderly would politely escort me to my position beside the head resident. And the service of deliverance would begin.

Somewhat reinvigorated by my new vision, I pushed open the doors of the delivery room and walked in, only to be greeted by—no one. I mean, not a soul. *Oh, no, I thought to myself, something has gone wrong with the delivery. They probably wheeled her up to surgery.*

I dashed out of the room and looked down the corridor. Nothing. Empty. Running down the hall in the direction of the nurses' station, I began to fear the worst. Maybe she had complications and they're doing a Caesarean section. Maybe they had to transfer her to another hospital and it happened too quickly for them to tell me. Maybe she already had the baby, and mother and child were already back in our apartment, straightening up the furniture. *Stupid idea, I thought to myself, they wouldn't operate or transfer her without my consent.*

When I reached the nurses' station, I was in a full state of panic. "Have you seen my wife and baby?" I panted. "I seem to have lost them."

The nurse sitting on the other side of the counter remained unmoved. In fact, except for her eyebrows (which arched a bit), her body remained totally inert. Ever so slowly, however, her eyes rolled over the top of her half-lens glasses and fixed their glare on me. "What are their names?" she said sternly.

"Judy Gaede," I responded quickly. "I don't know the name of the baby. In fact, I don't know if the baby's been born yet, so I don't know if it's a boy or girl, and we thought we'd wait on the gender to give—"

She held up the palm of her hand like a New York traffic cop stopping the flow of traffic. I obeyed. Ever so slowly, she ran her fingers down a list of names. "Nope," she said, "she hasn't been discharged." She got out a second piece of paper with a long list of names on it, and again leisurely slid her index finger down the list.

"Nope," she repeated, "she hasn't had the baby yet."
Calmly, she picked up the telephone and called the labor
room. "Nope," she said, after waiting for twenty-two
rings on the telephone, "she's not in the labor room."

"Ma'am," I interjected in an unusually high-pitched
voice, "could you check with—"

She approximated the policeman, once again, and
again she stopped me in my tracks. The index finger of
her right hand (which looked more powerful than a
locomotive) was again at work, running down the
various lists in front of her.

"Ah, huh!" she finally barked. "She's in the delivery
room."

"No Ma'am, she's not," I said, my voice now
reaching new levels of hushed intensity. "I was just in
the delivery room and no one's there—"

The hand stopped me again. "She's in the delivery
room, young man," she said emphatically, as she pointed
down the hall in the opposite direction from the one I
had come. "10-B," she added with a touch of triumph.

I noted the direction of her pointed finger and
realized I had two options. I could argue with her. Or I
could assume that I walked into the wrong delivery room
the first time and try to find 10-B by myself. The second
option seemed safer, certainly. And probably faster.

I ran down the hall again, this time without a holy
thought in the world, but with the sure expectation that I
had missed the event altogether. Judy's mother had had
very quick deliveries, I knew, and Judy had dilated
quickly herself. Chances are, the baby was born while the
locomotive was running down the second list of names.
Chances are, I missed out on the event of a lifetime.
Chances are . . .

A door with 10-B inscribed over it interrupted my
chain of despair. I paused in front of the room, once
again facing a swinging door, and once again wondering

what I would find on the other side. I plunged ahead, horrified at the possibilities but worried most of all that the room would again be empty.

It was not. Boy, was it ever not. Indeed, the room was teeming with people. Not only those attending the birth, but many others as well who were sitting in a gallery at one end of the room. We're talking ten rows of people, mind you; young women mostly, sitting behind a glass partition, in tiered church pews, on the birthing end of the delivery room. And here's the good part: When I walked into the room, the gallery broke into applause. For me!

Now, given what I had gone through, you might have expected that I would have been somewhat suspicious of this show of approval. That I would have assumed it was for someone else. Or that it was some form of mock approval, reprimanding me for my tardiness, or laughing at my attire. (I must admit, I did quickly look down to make sure the mask wasn't still around my waist). But I am not like that. When people applaud, I assume it is for me. Especially, when one of those offering approval is my wife, and when the same said wife—though only moments from giving birth—is giving me one of her "you're a prince" looks. In such circumstances, I'm a believer.

I took a slight bow then and strode casually to the seat reserved for me next to Judy's side. After giving C. Wright Mills a little wave, and acknowledging the presence of others, I leaned over next to Judy's ear, "What in the world are all these people doing here?" I whispered. "I haven't seen so many people in one room since our wedding."

She laughed. "I invited them, honey," she said. "They're students in the school of nursing. One of them mentioned to me that they were studying obstetrics in class and said they were hoping to see a live birth soon. I said, 'Great. Why don't you join us.' So, she okayed it with the doctor, the hospital changed delivery rooms, and here we are. Isn't it wonderful?"

"You bet," I said with a smile, thinking about what I had just been through for the last hour or so. "Couldn't be better."

I was lying, of course, but I shouldn't have been. It was wonderful. Aside from the moment when C. Wright Mills performed the episiotomy—at which time I assumed that our lovemaking days were gone forever—Heather's birth turned out to be one of the highlights of my life. Not for the way it looked. Not because we had such a grand team of medical people taking care of us. And not because we had the largest audience in the hospital's history. It was wonderful because, well . . . it's hard to explain.

I suppose I should start by telling you that I have never understood fathers who—to impress their friends with the wonder of childbirth—peel out reams of snapshots detailing every moment of their child's birth. Now, I am not opposed to slime. Blood doesn't bother me either, especially if it's not my own. And after seeing the birth of three children now, I am pretty much to the point where I can watch the enormous head of a baby slide though that diminutive little birth canal without hyperventilating (not unlike pulling your lower lip over your head, according to Carol Burnett).

But it doesn't seem like the kind of picture you'd want to hang over your dining room table, or show to your friends during lunch at Pizzeria Uno. Frankly, I wonder about fathers who spend the entire time their wives are stretching-their-lower-lips-over-their-heads taking pictures. I'm not real sure about their wives either, if you want to know the truth, though one suspects they have more important things to do than worry about their husband's voyeuristic proclivities.

Whatever the reasons for such behavior, and I'll admit that some of my best friends do it, it still seems to miss the point. Childbirth isn't wonderful because of the physiological details of the event. And the significance of the moment isn't caught by the facts of a yawning cervix, slimy blue babies, or mile-long umbilical cords. These are all fine and dandy, and even grand for the student of physiology, but they aren't really the decisive factors for the rest of us.

Nor is it the accoutrements of the occasion that retrieve it from the mundane. The rituals of modern medicine certainly are a spectacle to see. Indeed, surrounded by the lights, gloves, gowns, orders, language, technology, and whatnot, one can easily lose the significance of the birth itself. Like Christmas presents that overwhelm the Gift of Christmas, the shimmer of instruments and procedures can sometimes overshadow the end for which such instruments were devised. But I have witnessed births elsewhere; in one-room shacks, in four-bedroom suburban homes, and in bamboo houses on sticks. And with or without modern medicine, let me assure you, it is still a wonder to behold.

No, seeing the birth of your child isn't wonderful because of what you see, but because of what it is. The visuals are only a conduit to something much grander, something much more wonderful than anything observed. For beyond the facts of the event is the event itself. And the event itself is nothing less than holy. Holiness means something set apart, something special, something singularly uncommon. It is holy because we recognize that here God is doing something shocking and extraordinary.

And witnessing a birth is shocking. Creation always is. To see that inert little form begin to flail and cough and stretch and cry is stupefying in and of itself. But to think of that tiny infant in all its potentiality—well, it nearly takes your breath away. For who would believe that this flimsy little piece of blue flesh could grow up into a person like our C. Wright Mills, bright enough to grasp the details of centuries of medicine in only a few years of medical school and not forget the insights of a little sociology along the way?

I ask you again, who could believe that? I couldn't, I can tell you that. My first thought when I looked at our newborn wasn't, "Oh yes, we have an artist on our hands here, or maybe a mechanic, or a merchant." It was hard enough for me to believe that this little being could even survive, much less grow into a thriving adult.

It wasn't until the doctor put Heather in her mother's arms, in fact, that the idea of her future hit me full force: The mother had once been the daughter. Judy too had been such a child. My wife. My lover. The organizational whiz-kid of our household. The one who can make the most scurrilous Scrooge break into a smile at the drop of a hat. The one who can shower, wash, and clean house on the day she gives birth. That woman was once a baby such as ours.

How can that be, anyway? How is such a transformation possible? I'm not asking that in the scientific sense, certainly; I know how modern scientists describe the developmental process. But descriptions are not explanations. You don't explain an artist's work by describing the movement of each brush stroke that went into it. Nor do you explain a human being by describing the sequence of events that led up to it. The question is, how can a child become a woman? How can a sperm and egg become a human being? And how can a night in a seedy motel in San Jose culminate in someone like my Heather?

To such questions, there are no answers. Only screwy little theories, manufactured by one generation and discarded by the next. "Too puny," we keep saying. "There must be a better way of accounting for humanity." And so we keep looking. And not finding. And all the while, the miracle of creation keeps happening all around us. Staring us in the face. Staggering us by its implications. Confronting us with the limits of our own understandings. And pointing us, again, Elsewhere.

Why can't we see that anyway? Why isn't it obvious to all concerned? Why do we keep looking inward, hoping to find some great clue in ourselves?

I keep thinking of a young man, full of expectations about childbirth, running to-and-fro in the hospital, looking to have his expectations fulfilled, and finding nothing but frustrations and empty rooms. Finally, in desperation, he looks elsewhere for help, only to be confronted—not with an answer—but by a lethargic enumeration of all his past failings. And when he hears that, he bows his head in despair and nearly bolts for the door. But he's stuck. His search has revealed only the emptiness of his own expectations, the paucity of his own deeds. He decides to wait for an answer.

Finally, the moment of truth arrives, carried not on the wings of an angel, but by a messenger who looks like a Sherman tank, with a message that's just about as subtle. "You're looking for the right thing, young man, but you're going about it in the wrong way." Remembering the history of his own failings and longing to see his love, he puts his trust in the messenger. "What else can I do," he mutters to himself as he heads down the hall to the delivery room.

And, once again, just as it has happened a million times before, the messenger delivers. Delivers that which is wonderful. Delivers that which is beyond human explanation. And fulfills, finally, the only one of our young man's expectations worth fulfilling: delivering up the holy event of creation.

7

LIFE AS A
STUDENT

Knowledge

Gary Brown. I remember the first time I saw that name. It was on a list from the college registrar, identifying the students in one of my courses. The class was fairly large so I didn't spend much time studying the list. I knew there would be many students on it that I didn't know yet. And given the size of the class, not to mention the dimensions of the brain, I knew I wouldn't know them all by the end of the term. Disappointment.

But Gary's name stuck out only because it seemed so ordinary. Even dull. I suppose when you're raised with a surname like Gaede and a Christian name like Stanley, any name looks ordinary. But Gary Brown struck me as being especially pedestrian.

My opinion didn't change the first time I connected the name to a face either. Gary was a nice-looking chap, but he didn't stand out in any particular way. Sandy hair. Not tall. Kind of quiet. An ordinary student in an ordinary class. Nothing to break into my train of thought about. Not surprisingly, I didn't get to know him until halfway through the course.

The first thing that caught my attention was his

midterm exam. It was good. Not the best in class, but good. Good enough, certainly, to make a professor stand up and take notice. Added to the grade was the fact that Gary began asking questions in class. Not the familiar, "What do you mean by that, Dr. Gaede," type questions. But questions that probed and pushed and were unusually filled with personal care and concern: "If that's true, then how can you say . . ." Questions from the heart, in other words. Questions that any prof would die for.

But the "ordinary" label was finally stripped from Gary forever on the first day he walked into my office. It was late in the afternoon and I was in the process of reducing the mountain of mail on my desk (or filling up my trash container, whichever you prefer). The phone rang. It was Gary on the line. He asked if I was going to be in my office the next half hour. I said, "Sure," and then he asked if he could drop by. Stunned by this bit of civility, I responded, "Of course. Of course. I'll even stop reading my mail for you!"

I didn't understand the reason for the call, however, since it came during my regular office hours. *Why didn't he just come up to my office?* I thought. *Why did he call first, instead?*

I had my answer about ten minutes later when Gary knocked on the half-open door of my office. As I said, "Come in," I noticed that Gary was breathing hard and his face had turned a robust shade of blue. At first I thought that maybe he was sick. But his ready smile and eager eyes suggested differently. He was not sick. He was simply very tired. And his chest, which was disproportionately large for his body, was heaving greatly.

What I learned in the days to follow—not from Gary, but from his advisor—was that Gary Brown had a serious heart condition. A condition that he had had since birth and that resulted in very poor blood circulation. Constant treatment, numerous operations, and regular transfusions had enabled him to live much longer than his doctors thought possible. That Gary was alive at the age of twenty was a minor miracle. That he was living on campus, taking a full load of courses, and succeeding academically was nothing short of extraordinary.

As you can imagine, then, exertion of any kind was extremely tiring to Gary. Thus, the walk up to my third-floor office was a major undertaking. He had called ahead just to make sure his exertion wasn't going to be for nothing.

I can't really tell you the specifics of our conversation that afternoon in my office, since it was the first of many. I do recall that he was puzzled by a number of things I had said in class that day. And I remember thinking, after he repeated my comments back to me, that they seemed a bit of a puzzlement to me as well. But most of the time, I just sat there watching this young lad. Struggling to stop his chest from heaving. Trying to regain a normal breathing rate. Slowly getting his color back. And totally absorbed—not in the physical problems that had me nearly spellbound—but in the issues of the course.

They were the issues of life, as well. They always were. That I remember distinctly. I like to think that my courses are full of such weighty matters; that they are not the mere presentation of disembodied facts. But I also know that the connection between course material and life is ultimately up to the student. I can't do that for them. They have to bring it home. To give it meaning. To make it live. In the end, only the student can turn knowledge into wisdom.

And Gary seemed to make the transformation easily.

Not all students do, I'm afraid. Sometime later, I had the privilege of giving a student the final exam of her college career. She had received an "incomplete" in one of my courses the term before. And now—just before the date that grades were due—she was hurriedly trying to make up the work that she had missed. So she could finish the one class that remained hanging over her head. So she could finally graduate from college.

She was not a bad student. At times, her work showed flashes of insight and real ability. On the whole, her grades were fairly good, reflecting the fact that she was naturally gifted. But they certainly were not as good as they could have been. And her transcript was laced with withdrawals and incompletes. In short, she was a better-than-average student turning in an average performance. And most importantly to her, she was getting by.

"Well, how did you like the book?" I asked, as I attempted to get the oral exam started off on an informal note.

"Not very," she said with a moan of despair, while her face assumed the posture of one who had just consumed a bottle of Pepto-Bismol.

"Not very what?" I asked, feigning linguistic innocence.

She shrugged her shoulders, not wanting to be too direct with the professor who had assigned the book. "I didn't like the book very much, Dr. Gaede. It just seemed that the author was saying the same old thing in a thousand different ways. I don't know," she shrugged, "I just don't get it."

"What didn't you get?" I pursued.

"I don't get the point of the book," she continued. "I mean, he just seems to be saying that Protestants are greedy capitalists, or something like that. And he says it in about fifteen hundred ways. What's the point, anyway. I mean, everybody knows that already, right?"

I paused for a moment, not knowing whether to laugh, shout, or cry. The book she was talking about is *The Protestant Ethic and the Spirit of Capitalism* by Max Weber. It is the classic statement concerning the relationship of Western capitalism and the development of Protestantism. It is a controversial book because of its premise, but it is cogently argued, easily read, and extraordinarily important to any student of sociology. And the one thing Weber tries to make clear, above all else, is that he is not saying that Protestants are greedy.

"I think you missed something," I said, deliberately understating the magnitude of the problem in order to regain my emotional equilibrium. "Do you remember what Weber said about Calvin's view of . . ." And off I went, trying to correct a misreading of Weber and promptly forgetting that I was the one who was supposed to be quizzing her, not vice versa.

I rambled on for some time before I realized that our hour was coming to a close, and I had learned almost nothing about my student's understanding of the book. Or maybe I had. Or maybe there wasn't much to learn. *Probably both,* I thought to myself somewhat cynically. *Oh well,* I continued talking to myself, *I'll find out what she knows from her written work on Weber.*

I decided to change the subject. It was our last time together, after all, and this was her last class. It was time to lighten up a bit.

"Well, tell me," I said with the smile of a friend rather than the scowl of a professor. "What do you plan to do with your life now?"

"I'm not sure," she said rather quickly. "Stop reading, I guess. In fact, I hope I don't ever see another book again for the rest of my life. I've had it with studying. I just want to go someplace and veg out for a while. I want to enjoy life for a change."

The words were said with lightheartedness. And I knew she was overstating her case. Using hyperbole for effect. But she couldn't have cut me more deeply if she had impaled me with a sword.

We continued to talk about superficial matters for a

while, until she finally said good-bye and walked out the door. But in my mind I just couldn't stop replaying the words I had heard only moments before. "Stop reading," I mumbled to myself. "Stop reading! What had I taught her anyway? Rejecting sociology, that's one thing; there's a lot there to reject, after all. Rejecting me, I could even take that. But reading and learning and growing? Hadn't I at least communicated the value of that in my classes? Had she rejected that gift as well?"

In deep despair, I pushed myself out of my chair and headed down to the dean's office, where fresh coffee is always kept brewing for moments such as this. It was final exam time, however, and the coffee pot had been completely drained. Apparently a lot of faculty were having moments like mine, I thought to myself.

And then I looked up at the bulletin board that sits just to the right of the coffee maker. And noticed that an announcement had been freshly posted.

"Dear Faculty," it began. "We have just learned that Gary Brown died of heart failure today. The time and place of the funeral have not yet been determined. Please pray for his family. . . ."

Wisdom

Gary Brown died only a few months after he graduated from college. He had gone a "fer piece" farther down the road than anyone thought he could. And upon his graduation from college, the hospital that had witnessed this feat—and given him support along the way—established a fund in Gary's name. They wanted to honor his courage and help others in short supply.

What is it that makes a student like Gary anyway? And what accounts for students like INGTRA, my I'm-never-going-to-read-again senior? Those were the questions that immediately bubbled to the surface that day in the coffee room and plagued me for the rest of the week as well.

The day Gary entered college, he knew there was a good chance he wouldn't live to see his own graduation. The primary reason most young people trot off to college these days—to secure a good job—was not his. Oh, I'm sure he dreamed of a career. I suspect that college was part of his career dreaming process. But the idea that college was simply a stepping-stone for success—a ticket to ride—that idea was foreign to him.

And its foreignness was evident in everything he did. It certainly was apparent in the kinds of conversations we had. Most students are concerned with one of two things when they walk into my office. Either they are worried about an upcoming exam; they want to know what they should do in order to get a good grade (answer: study). Or they are concerned about a former exam; they want to know what they can do about a low grade they have already received (answer: nothing).

I remember few such conversations with Gary, however. What I recall, instead, were discussions about life. About the importance of course material for the way we live our lives. About the truthfulness of what was read. About the relevance of what was learned. About the meaning of what we know. About the implications of what we don't know. In sum, they were discussions not merely about knowledge but about the relationship between what we know and what we do. They were discussions, in other words, about wisdom.

INGTRA was not looking for wisdom. And I'm sure she found exactly what she was looking for. Isn't that a pity? She is the one with a healthy body and a long life in front of her. She is the one who will enter the marketplace and confront the ethical dilemmas there. She is the one who will marry and face the task of rearing children in the modern world. She is the one who will vote and teach and serve. And not serve. She is the one who will love her neighbor as herself. And not love. She is the one who will take the Gospel of Jesus Christ to the ends of the earth. And not . . .

What a pity. What a disappointment. And sadly, she is in the majority. At technical schools. At elite universities. At state colleges. Even at colleges of the liberal arts. She is the student that is filling up most of our classrooms these days. She is pleasant. She is kind. She is easy to talk to and easy to like. But the connection between the mind and the heart simply hasn't been made.

You cannot teach students like Gary and INGTRA without asking the question: Why? Why are the Garys like precious gems, rare and rarely discovered? Why are the INGTRAs like summer mosquitoes in Minnesota, ubiquitous beyond belief?

It isn't because they are heartless, that's for sure. Many of the students I come into contact with deeply love the Lord and are vitally concerned about others. They wear their affections on their sleeves, and it's not hard to discover whether they are happy or sad, glad or mad. Working with them, moreover, is an absolute joy. I love my students not only because I make a point of doing so but because they are easy to love. I wouldn't trade their hearts for all the diamonds in Johannesburg.

It isn't because they're dumb, either. I am routinely impressed by the intellectual capacity of the average collegian, especially when that capacity is provoked by a stimulating idea or interesting personality. True, many students come to college with academic deficiencies (especially in math and writing skills). But even those who struggle are often very bright. Their lack of performance results more from weak training than weak minds. Ability, in my experience, is not the problem.

The minds and the hearts, then, seem to be in fairly good shape. But for some reason the connection between the two just isn't being made. Why is that? To this question many answers can be given. Answers about the way we raise children, the way we have designed our educational system, the way we teach our teachers, and so on.

But I want to suggest that modern students have this connection problem primarily because, like us, they are modern people. The difficulty is not merely that they are young or undisciplined or listen to rock music or whatever. The problem is not that they are different than us, but the same. And the most important similarity is how they think. Or more precisely, how our world has taught them to think.

One of the most significant developments in the modern world is the separation of knowledge from action. Of knowing from doing. We learn, from a very early age, that there is a time for learning and a time for acting. And that the relationship between the two is tenuous at best.

Like the rest of you, I went to school at the age of five. School, I was told, is the place where I would learn. And the first separation was made: Learning occurs at school; other things happen at home. Before long, the school day was divided up into sections, with history lessons coming at one point, literature coming at another, and recess sandwiched in between. And thus came separation number two: The things you learn are distinct from each other, and from play.

By the time I was in high school I was learning things my parents didn't know and my grandparents had never heard of. And yet, they were living very productive lives without this knowledge. If I happened to ask why I was studying what I was studying, a few brave teachers would try to explain it. But the majority simply said, "You'll need it in trigonometry," or "constitutional history." Or, "You'll need it in order to get into college." And suddenly, separation number three was performed: Learning is simply a means to an end, a way to get more knowledge, a way to gain success.

What was lost in all of this was not only the joy and meaning of learning itself, but the idea that knowledge is an integral part of life. That knowing had something to do with doing. And the more specialized my studies became, the deeper the chasm grew. First, in college.

And then in graduate school. By the time I earned my
Ph.D., I was a specialist in fragmentation.

Lest you are tempted to think that the problem is
simply "the educational system," let me hasten to add
that modern education is designed to suit the modern
world. The fragmentation one finds there is duplicated in
spades in the marketplace. The reason education is
confined to the classroom, moreover, is to make it more
streamlined, more efficient, more democratic, and more
suited to the needs of modern jobs.

Whatever the reasons, however, the effect is that
today we tend to reward people for what they know, not
for what they do with what they know. And the easiest
thing in the world to become in our society is an
irresponsible knower. To watch the news and yawn. To
study the statistics on abortion and say, "That's interesting, they've doubled this year." To study the poverty in
urban America and build an equation to explain it. And
in the end, to study whatever it is we're studying and
say, "Who cares? What's it for?" And conclude, in the
words of INGTRA, "I'm never going to read another book
again as long as I live."

How different this is from the biblical picture of
knowledge. Where knowing is doing. And where knowing, and not doing, is a sin. "Dear children, let us not
love with words or tongue but with actions and in truth.
This then is how we know that we belong to the truth"
(1 John 3:18). Simply stated, the truth of what we know
is made apparent in the actions that proceed from it.
Those who know but don't act are condemned; their
knowledge is worthless in the eyes of our Lord (Matt. 25).

Indeed, a case can be made that knowing without
doing isn't knowing at all. When Abraham knew his
wife, Sarah, what happened? Did he study her? Did he
measure her dimensions and develop an equation to
explain them? Well, maybe so, and it would not have

been wrong for him to do so (as long as Sarah didn't mind). But when Abraham knew Sarah he made love to his wife and conceived a nation. *Conceived* a nation. Thinking and doing are one.

We know this, of course. In our moments of candor, we know that the fragmentation of knowledge is utter nonsense. But rarely do we live as if it were so. And rarely do we design our homes, our classrooms, our churches, or our governments as if it were so. Especially those of us in the modern world, where fragmentation is usually assumed to be an absolute good.

In the end, however, the problem is not the classroom or government or society; the problem is us. These environments only make irresponsible knowledge easier. They don't make it inevitable. The decision not to act on what we know is ours. It is the choice we sinners like to make. It not only suits our circumstances, it suits our nature as well.

Gary Brown made that abundantly clear. He too lived in the modern world. He lived in the midst of our schools. Our economies. Our circumstances. And yet he lived differently. And his approach to living was evident in the way he thought about things. In the kind of student he was.

The difference, of course, was that Gary lived with the reality of death. That reality paralyzes some, but for Gary, it only heightened his sense of what mattered. And what mattered to him as a student was that he learned, not merely memorized. That he understood, not merely knew. That he grew in wisdom, not merely knowledge. And so, in a few short years, Gary learned more than most of us learn in a lifetime. And lived a lot longer.

Oh, Lord, send us more Garys.

8

LIFE AS A
PARENT

Humility

Why does the Lord give us children? That is the question. Is it so we can witness the thrill of childbirth? Is it so that we can have the privilege of watching our children mature? Is it so that we might one day have little grandchildren to spoil . . . and then happily give them back to their parents, who must then live with them?

No. In all these things we are more than conquerors. Far more likely, it seems to me, is the possibility that God gives us children to keep us humble. For certainly humility is the most universal consequence of parenthood. And the degree of humility that one can learn from being a dad knows no bounds.

A number of years ago, when my son Nathaniel was only five, he and I were driving up to Ipswich to pick up a pizza. Now Ipswich is only six or seven miles from our house, so this wasn't an extremely long journey. It was long enough, however, for Nathaniel to say something that irritated me.

I can't even recall what he said. My guess is that I was very hungry, in desperate need of a pizza, and thus probably a little more irritable than normal. I also suspect

131

that Nathaniel, being only five at the time, probably made one of those comments that five-year-olds are prone to make, like, "Dad, what's that hanging from your nose?" or, "Why don't you have any hair on the back of your head?"

Whatever he said, it irked me, so I did what dads often do under pressure: I unleashed my weapon of choice, which in this case happened to be my tongue. I lectured him on manners. I lectured him on sensitivity to the feelings of others. I threw the Golden Rule at him (a strange thing to do, given what it means, but I did it anyway), and I'm sure I threw out every other Bible verse I could think of as well. In other words, picture a father who has completely lost control—who is moving down the track of self-righteous criticism, with a full head of steam and no interest whatsoever in listening to anyone else's opinions or ideas.

Well, eventually, I ran out of steam. When I finished my harangue, Nathaniel didn't say a word. He sat there beside me in the car, looking out the window, silently staring into space. Now you have to understand that this isn't Nathaniel's way. He's a real talker normally, and usually when I rip into him like that, he responds with a few verbal punches of his own. So I was quite surprised when he just sat there and said nothing.

This went on for quite a while—Nathaniel gazing blankly out into space and me sitting there thinking, *Wow, I must have really gotten through to him this time. The old man really delivered the knockout blow.*

Eventually, the silence was broken by his calm, dispassionate voice. "You know what, Dad?" he said with conviction. "When I grow up, I think I want to live all by myself on top of a mountain."

Wham! With one little comment my inflated sense of self-righteousness was gone, popped with the pin of five-year-old honesty. I had said everything that needed to be said. I had delivered tons and tons of truth, backed up by Scripture, and driven it all home with the force of a cattle prod. And what had all my truth telling accomplished? Not changed behavior. Not new insight into moral responsibility. Not, "Wow, Dad, you're right! I need to be sensitive to others. From now on, I'll be good." No. It resulted instead in a five-year-old boy who would rather live alone on the top of a mountain for the rest of his life than listen to his father.

I sat there for a few minutes without saying a word. I couldn't. I didn't know what to say. Finally, I did my best to offer an apology. "I, uh, I guess I overdid it just a bit this time, didn't I, Nathaniel?" And then—probably just to emphasize the fact that he was a lot nicer then me— Nathaniel looked over and smiled. Then he slipped across to my side of the car, put his arm around me, and gave me a big hug. I mean, not only does the guy have to teach me humility, but he gives me a lesson on forgiveness at the same time.

And me? I sat there, with my arm now around my son, and thought how blessed I was that God gave me a child such as this. And I wondered, how much more humility can I take? How much more humble, Lord, do I have to become?

The answer, apparently, is a great deal more. Because not long after that, Nathaniel and I were again together, this time at a shopping mall, and this time doing a little Christmas shopping. Now you must understand that I dislike shopping intensely. The crowds bother me for one thing. I'm slightly claustrophobic, and the thought of being crowded together with ten million people in Filene's basement gives me the heebie-jeebies.

But there is more to it than that. I simply don't have the intelligence or emotional stamina to be a good shopper. Shopping is one long series of disappointments, as far as I can tell. Even if you do it right—if you sit down, make a list of the things you want to buy and where you want to buy them, and then methodically go out to make your purchases—even if you do that, you'll be frustrated.

Some items you want to purchase won't be there; and if they are, they're not in the right color, size, or price. And then you must make a decision: Should I buy the nightgown anyway, even if it's purple and she hates purple? Maybe I should get a negligee instead. She likes red. I like red! But she doesn't need a negligee. But I need the negligee! But you're not buying her a Christmas present to suit your needs; it's her needs you're trying to meet. Okay then, what do I buy her?

So you grab the purple nightgown, which you know she needs but you know she will hate, and you go to the cashier and stand in line for forty-five minutes—which means you have 2,500 seconds to contemplate the ugly purple nightgown that you're buying for your favorite person in the whole world. By the time you get to the cash register, therefore, you've had it. You bolt from the line, throw the purple nightgown down, and make for the door. Getting out of the store, you feel like a wild stallion that's just been released from a year of bondage. There is nothing you want more than to run free with the wind, away from people, stores, and Christmas presents.

But then in your mind's eye you see the image of your family sitting around the Christmas tree, no presents, no laughter, no music. Just the sight of your five-year-old, staring at you sternly, saying, "Read my lips: YOU are the Grinch that stole Christmas!"

And so, tail between your legs, you do the thing you want more than anything else in the world not to do, you head back to the store. Back into bondage. Back to find a better Christmas present.

Well, that was my emotional state on the day that Nathaniel and I were shopping. I was exhausted, exasperated, and deeply depressed. To give us a lift, therefore, we decided to have a little pizza for lunch (you can see that pizza is a major theme in our family; some families ski together; others go camping; we eat pizza). One of the consequences of pizza, however—especially if you're only five years old—is slime: gooey, greasy, tomato sauce all over one's mouth, hands, and parts unknown.

To handle the slime problem, Nathaniel and I made our way to the public restroom, where we wanted merely to wash our hands and face, and leave in peace. When we walked into the bathroom, however, we were confronted not only with the usual sights and smells of a public facility, but with water faucets of a somewhat unusual nature. These were not the normal faucets you grew up with, where you simply turn the handle counterclockwise. These were the kind you often find in public washrooms these days; you push the top down and then water trickles from the spout—until, of course, you get your hands under the water, by which time it stops. This means that you can have water running from the faucet or have your hands under the faucet, but you can't have both at the same time.

Well, I had had experience with these kinds of faucets before. And I also had a Ph.D. So naturally I came up with a brilliant solution to the problem. I asked Nathaniel to join me at one basin and work with me to wash our hands. The plan was simple. Nathaniel would push the knob releasing the water, and I would then be able to wash both my hands at the same time. This plan was predicated upon the assumption that one would want to have the faucet on for a sustained length of time. At least, that's what I told Nathaniel. "Don't let go of the button," I implored. "Keep pushing until I have finished washing my hands."

Well, Nathaniel certainly did his part. He pushed

that button with all his might, and for an extended length of time. Unfortunately, the faucet required no such encouragement and proceeded to release a torrent only marginally shy of an Amazonian cloudburst. I immediately shouted for Nathaniel to let go of the button, of course, but he seemed to prefer my former instruction to this new command. And so the water kept coming. I kept yelling. And in the end Nathaniel was left with slime on his hands and I was left with a huge water spot covering the entire midsection of my body.

After an incident of this kind, there are many things one wants to do. Strangling a plumber seemed like a good idea, for example, or perhaps a son who believes in following the letter of the law and not its spirit. But given the fact that I was soaking wet, I decided that the first thing I ought to do was dry off.

At that moment I encountered the second interesting thing about the restroom: it had no hand towels. There were dispensers, of course, but they were empty, as were the toilet paper rolls in the stalls nearby. The only drying agent in the room, therefore, was a hot-air machine, located on the back wall and operated by—you guessed it—another little button.

Well, this time I was prepared. I told Nathaniel to stand back; that I would operate the hot-air machine by myself. I approached it carefully, gently touched the button, and to my surprise, a powerful but entirely appropriate stream of hot air proceeded to emanate from the machine. I immediately began to dry my hands.

I had another problem, however. You will recall that not only my hands were wet but also the midsection of my body. The question became: What do I do about my soaking wet pants? I quickly glanced around the bathroom. Except for Nathaniel, it was empty. Once again, therefore, I carefully approached the air machine, pushed the magic button, and redirected the flow of air to my midsection by turning the nozzle downward.

I stood there a moment letting the hot air do its thing, feeling rather good about my solution, and feeling rather good about the hot air as well, when I suddenly turned to see a gentleman standing in the entryway of the rest room, watching my performance. His expression was somewhere between astonishment and moral outrage, and so—realizing my rather compromising position—I quickly backed away from the hot-air machine, gave the man a little wave, and started for the exit.

Unfortunately, Nathaniel did not. Instead, he had become fascinated with the nozzle of the hot-air machine, which (from watching me) he had discovered could move in various directions. As I backed away, Nathaniel moved right in, grabbing the nozzle with one hand and pushing it toward the side with the other, and inadvertently aiming the flow of hot air directly at the man who had been watching me.

Now there is one more thing you need to know about this bathroom. Located between the hot-air machine and the man standing in the entryway was a cigarette disposal unit, filled to the brim with sand. When Nathaniel aimed the nozzle of the machine at the man in the entryway, he blasted the man—not only with hot air—but with a significant quantity of sand as well, not to mention cigarette butts, ashes, gum, and whatever else people stuff into those containers.

For a moment, the man looked like Lawrence of Arabia in a sandstorm. Except he wasn't dressed for the occasion. Nor was he particularly pleased to be there. Lawrence always seemed to love the sand, you know; this man did not. Instead of appreciating the experience, he simply whirled around on one foot and headed right back out the door, probably to seek help from the local police.

Nathaniel and I didn't stick around to find out. We hightailed it out of the bathroom; me, calmly engaged in another one of my brilliant lectures; Nathaniel, crying at the top of his lungs; and everyone else, watching and probably wondering, "Why can't that man control his son—or his bladder, for that matter?" I was left with a different question, however: Why me, Lord? What did I do to deserve this? What evil, awful, low, scummy, nasty thing did I do, somewhere in my youth or childhood, to deserve this kind of humiliation?

Finitude

Upon reflection it is clear that mine was a silly response. For one thing, my humiliation wasn't that unusual. Every dad has experiences of this kind. Being a dad entails being a fool at times. And I really had no reason to think that I was being uniquely persecuted that day in the shopping mall.

Moreover, I have discovered that such feelings of frustration quickly vanish in the warp and woof of daily parenting. For every bad experience there are an equal number of good ones. And the good ones seem to nestle themselves more closely to the heart. You don't forget them easily. In all honesty, one child, running into my arms when I get home and saying with a big grin, "Hi, Dad," is enough to wipe away every bad memory from the face of the earth.

That fact, however, raises a rather serious question about everything I have said up to this point. If the good experiences are so precious, so wonderful, so memorable, then what is the point of raising all these negative experiences? Aren't they just momentary lapses in the

scheme of things? Do they have any enduring significance? Are they even worth pondering?

Well, I think they are. And the reason is that they
serve as useful reminders of two very important truths;
truths that are made self-evident in the experiences of
parenting, but truths that we very much need to hear if
we want to think and act Christianly in the modern
world. First, regardless of what I do as a parent, my
children will behave in ways that will surprise me. And
second, their surprising behavior will sometimes make
me rejoice and sometimes make me cry, but it will
always remind me that I am not God.

Now why would we need to be reminded of these
truths anyway? That's a good question. Because, after all,
they are obvious to anyone who has taken up the grand
enterprise of parenting. And they should be obvious to
any inhabitant of planet earth, shouldn't they? Humans
around us are not tame. Those that we know on the most
intimate level continue to do things that totally astound
us. And we—whether we are parents, employers, super-
visors, teachers, or in any other way exercise responsibility over the lives of others—we know fundamentally that
we are not in control, that our authority is always
tentative, always temporary, and always subject to
change. Given these obvious facts, then, why in the
world do we need to be reminded of them?

I think the answer is this: We live with a worldview
that contradicts the experiences of everyday life. Though
people are a surprise to us daily, our worldview says they
shouldn't be. Though our children do not perform
precisely as we want them to, our worldview says they
ought to. And so it is that we keep on believing that we
can totally understand one another and control one
another, in spite of the fact that there is little evidence to
support that conclusion.

Now when a worldview has this kind of power—

when something can be believed in spite of, not because of the evidence—then we know that we are confronting something deep within us and within our culture. And certainly that is the case here. Because it is a fundamental assumption within the modern worldview that we human beings are or can be gods. We don't talk about it this way, certainly. It would be offensive to some, and clearly not palatable language to the average Christian. But our language does betray us, nevertheless.

Listen to the way we talk sometimes. Listen for the word "I" especially, and notice how it is used to justify behavior.

Why do you go to Oak Street Church? Because I enjoy the way the pastor preaches; I like it there; I find comfort there.

Why did you decide to abort your baby? Because I wasn't ready for a child yet.

Why did you decide to have a baby? Because I want to see what it's like to be a parent, to hold a baby, to have someone call me "Daddy."

Why did you accept that job? Because I could make more money.

Why did you turn down that job offer? Because I didn't think I would be happy there.

And we could go on and on. Nearly everything we do or don't do these days is justified in terms of personal fulfillment. In fact, we take this so much for granted that we find it difficult to answer these questions any other way. Who accepts a job so that they can serve others? Who has a child or remains childless out of responsibility or duty? Who attends a church because they can minister there or serve God's people there or worship God there?

In point of fact, we have gotten comfortable with the language of self-fulfillment because we have gotten comfortable with the modern worldview. And at the heart of that worldview is the assumption that I am the most important thing in the universe. That my needs come first. That my happiness is all that ultimately matters. The fact that such a worldview blatantly contradicts Scripture, from beginning to end, seems not to matter a whit. What matters is "me" and what counts is how I feel.

Now when the self replaces God at the center of the universe, some interesting things begin to happen. The most important, for this discussion, is that people begin to order their world according to their own wants and aspirations. This, of course, is a difficult thing to do since the people around them are doing the same thing, and since a great many things happen that are not in the least predictable. Nevertheless, the self is not easily deterred. It demands fulfillment. And fulfillment requires control. You cannot guarantee your own happiness unless you are able to control events and manage people.

To a large extent, this explains why millions of books are written every year about managing people, raising children, handling mates, directing careers, growing churches, controlling whatever. And every year we purchase these books, in spite of the fact that the advice rarely works; in spite of the fact that we have already purchased ten books before on the same topic.

Why do we do that? Why do we keep investing our money in projects that are doomed from the start? Because, frankly, we find the promise of control absolutely irresistible. What these books dangle before our eyes is precisely what our worldview says is the most important thing imaginable: control over our careers. Control over our churches. Control over our spouses. Control over our children. Control over our God.

But God cannot be controlled. And he would be within his rights to either ignore our attempts at control or simply push us and our petty little pretensions aside. But thanks be to God, he is not like that. Instead, out of his grace and mercy he periodically reminds us of the folly of our ways. And one way that he has done this in my life is through my children.

I came to parenthood with the assumptions of my age. I thought they were biblical. I had learned many of them in church, in fact. I had learned, for example, that good Christian parents ought to raise good Christian children. I had heard the verse, "Raise up your child in the way he should go, and when he is old he will not depart from it," and I had assumed it meant that responsible parents can make their children turn out the way they want them to turn out.

Ignored in all of this, of course, was the fact that I had responsible parents and I didn't turn out the way they had planned. Ignored too was the fact that few children in my church were duplicating the patterns set out by their parents for them, yet they had responsible parents. Ignored, most of all, was the biblical picture of humanity, which—from beginning to end—shows human beings to be choosing creatures; who make choices within the context of God's sovereign will, not their own; and for good as well as ill, do all kinds of unexpected things.

Ignored, finally, was the obvious fact that "raising a child in the way he should go" referred not to the way the parent wanted the child to go, but the way God intended for the child to go; that the parents' responsibility was to honor God in their child-rearing practices, not to honor themselves.

All of this I ignored, not because I was stupid, but because I was gullible. When the world whispered in one ear, "You are the master of your own fate," I winced a little, but I wanted to believe. But when the church chimed in the other, "God wants you to be happy, all

you've got to do is think positively and go for the gold"—
that I couldn't resist. Nor did I want to. And so I went out
there, like a good little boy, to make my fortune, do my
thing, and bring my world into line with my needs and
requirements, and have perfect children.

But God was good. He did not let me do my own
thing. And through a whole host of events and experiences—not the least of which was being a dad—God
finally confronted me with a truth I had known all along,
but just couldn't get myself to admit:

"Stan," he said, "you are not God. I did not ask that
of you in the first place, nor do I ask that of you now. You
do not exercise sovereignty over your own life, much less
the lives of others. And there is no reason for you to
pretend otherwise. Remember, I have called you to serve,
not to be served. To proclaim my truth, not to claim your
own. To honor me, not to seek honor for yourself. Go and
do what I have commanded. And let me, the Sovereign
God of human history, worry about the consequences."

Worrying about the consequences. That's the rub,
isn't it? At least it is for me. Because the consequences
are what people see. Nobody sees the hard work you put
into a project. Nobody sees the time you spend with your
children. Nobody knows the hours you spend thinking
about your workplace. Nobody sees the labor you put
into a church program. What people see is the grades
your children earn in school or how they behave during
the morning worship service. What people see is your
production rate at work or your program's implementa-
tion at church. What people see is the results of your
efforts. And those results? Well, they are often not what
you had hoped they would be.

You work on manners with your children till you're
blue in the face and then the minute you get to church,
your children lose all sense of common decency, slouch
in their seats, snort during the sermon, and climb over

the tops of pews in order to make a fast exit after the benediction. You toil late into the night, working out the details of a new approach to sales, and the next day you find out that the sales force has been cut in half and your new approach can't be implemented. You pour yourself into a Sunday-school lesson for the senior-high youth group, but when you present it, the kids just yawn or chew gum or worse.

And you cry out into the darkness, Lord, why me? Or in the words I used after the incident in the public bathroom, "What did I do to deserve this? What awful, evil, scummy thing did I do somewhere in my youth or childhood to justify this?"

And the Lord? Well, the Lord must just shake his head in wonder. "Why do you think you have absolute control over your children, Stan? Did I not create them, as well as you? Why should your salespeople act according to your plans, Bill? And why should the senior-high youth group behave the way you expected them to, Judy? And most importantly of all—Stan and Bill and Judy—why do you say that 'nobody sees the hard work you put into the project'? I see. Am I nobody?

"I have seen whether you honored me in the way you have treated your children, doesn't that count? I have seen the service you have offered—at work or at church or in your neighborhood—isn't that enough? Why must you have your honor, your treasure on earth, where moth and rust destroy, and thieves break through and steal? Isn't it better for your treasure to be stored with me, where it is safe, and where it will be yours to enjoy forever? Wouldn't you rather live with me for an eternity, than pretend you are a god for a little while, right now?"

Yes, Lord, we would. And, thanks be to you and the salvation you have offered us through Jesus Christ, we will. But in the meantime, Father, we need reminders. I need reminders. And so we are thankful for the reminders you give us daily in the form of our children. Reminders, first, of your generosity, for children are a gift from you. But reminders, as well, of our finitude, or our place in this world which you have created. Reminders that we are stewards of your creation, not its gods. Reminders that we tend the seeds that you have sown, but we do not determine the plant's growth. Reminders that our final duty is to honor you through our acts of service to one another, not to serve and honor ourselves.

May God grant us the wisdom
to be parents whose treasure
lies in heaven
and not in the applause of others.

9

LIFE AS A COMPANION

Strangers

To live in the modern world is to live among strangers. That was not always the case. For most of human history, people lived in relatively small communities, did not travel far, and knew most of those around them. Today it's quite the opposite. Our towns are not communities, nor are they small. We move frequently, and we know only a tiny fraction of those we see in an average day.

Most of us have gotten used to living among strangers. We simply ignore other people, unless we need them or recognize someone as a friend. We drive along the freeway, passing hundreds of unique faces, but we rarely even notice. Periodically someone striking comes along, and we think, "pretty," or "nice," or "ugh." But these remain just faces, caricatures really, standards against which we judge ourselves. We do not relate to them as people.

For this reason, when we do suddenly spot an acquaintance on the highway, it is a jolt comparable to being caught with our pants down. We are embarrassed by our own demeanor. And quickly, we must change from being aloof observers to caring friends and communicators. We must try to look human again.

Those of us who were raised in small towns bear a particular burden in all of this, I think. We grew up thinking of people as people but, in short order, had to learn differently. It is a transition rural folks find difficult to make and urbanites find difficult to understand.

Have you ever been traveling out in the sticks, stopped at a gas station, and found people staring at you? It isn't something one notices right away. But about the time the fourth gallon enters your tank and you've finally found your credit card, you glance up only to discover some fellow leaning against the doorway or sitting on the porch next door, looking at you with all the subtlety of a stuffed pig. If you catch his eye, he may look away, but not likely. And if he does, it's only momentary. In a matter of seconds, his eyes will be back in your direction, and they will stay there until you have driven far beyond the horizon.

This habit makes urbanites go berserk, and they are likely to chalk it up to inbreeding: too many cousins marrying too many cousins producing too many offspring who stare blankly for exercise. That's a possible explanation, I suppose, but not likely correct. In all probability, the starer has an IQ to match the staree. What the starer has not learned, however, is how to ignore people. Especially people from out of town, who don't look others in the eye and who act as if gasoline is more important than the person filling the tank. That's interesting to the starer. And worth puzzling over.

Even small towners who have lived in the city for years find people-watching difficult to resist. In a subway, they keep looking up from their newspapers. Walking along the sidewalk, they can't help catching the eyes of other pedestrians. Sitting in the park, they find themselves reading other people as often as they read

their own novels. For these breaches of etiquette, however, they pay a price, feeling guilty one day for not
complying with the standards of civilization, feeling
guilty the next for doing so. And always feeling a bit
lonely because no one looks back.

That was my mood the evening Judy, Heather, and I
stopped at Shakey's Pizza Parlor on Beach Boulevard.
We were on vacation and had spent the entire day at the
ocean. Heather, who was only three, had had a great
time, of course. And Judy, who was three-going-on-
twenty-six and always enjoys a chance to lay on the sand
and put her toes in the water, had also found the day
exhilarating. For the two of them the beach was a grand
experience. A break from the routine. A chance to relax.

For me, the beach had been a pain in the neck. I love
the ocean, ordinarily. I love the smell of it, the sound of
it, the look of it, and the feel of it on a hot summer day.
Walking along the shore at dusk, body surfing in the
afternoon, sailing in the morning—these are nearly
religious experiences for me. The power and beauty of
the Creator are no more evident than when one is in, on,
or around the ocean.

But there is one thing that happens at the ocean that
I have never been able to understand, nor fully appreciate, and that is the phenomenon of *lying* on the beach.
Why do people do that, anyway? Now, I'll admit that
there is a moment or two when the hot sun feels good:
that somewhere between the impossible task of contour-
ing your body to the lumpy sand and retrieving the first
speck of sand out of your eye, there is a moment of
genuine pleasure. But it never lasts long. And the price
for that ecstasy seems extraordinarily high.

I suppose it could be argued that there is a certain
visual benefit to the beach. Rarely does one get the
chance to see so much skin, after all, and of course the
ocean is there in all its magnificent glory. But these

benefits are also illusory, I think. Most people that I see at the beach really shouldn't be there. Or at least, I shouldn't be looking at them. And the few who do look good in a swimsuit serve only as reminders of failed exercise regimens, failed diets, failed bodies. As for the ocean, who can see it amidst all the humanity? Or hear it, amidst all the boom boxes? Or smell it amidst all the concession stands?

In the meantime, one has to put up with so much. Sand, which is a fine thing to look at or walk on, makes a perfectly awful bed. I can't imagine that God thought people over seven years old would ever want to lie on it. Time is also a problem at the beach. Some people read, but I find that the sun is always too bright, the sand too uncomfortable, and the heat too energy-sapping to carry on a quality relationship with a book. So once the swimming is over, I wind up just lying there, soaking in cancer and waiting for the inevitable headache to begin. Not good.

Finally, there is the thing that I find most depressing of all: the utter anonymity of the beach on a holiday. Especially in Southern California—where the beaches are long and the people are legion—the beach is a sea of strangers. People lying side by side, revealing intimate body parts to one another but absolutely nothing else. When I'm all alone, walking down a craggy New England beach at dawn, I feel close to God, close to his creation, and even close to those unknowns who sometimes cross my path. But lying on a beach in the summer amidst 15 million sun worshipers, I am totally alone.

As we walked into Shakey's, therefore, I was not in a good mood. Nor by that time was anyone else if I remember correctly. Even if you like the beach, coming home from it is a dismal experience. But more than likely, in my crankiness I had even managed to sour the day for my wife and daughter as well. Whatever the

reason, tempers were short. Conversations were accusa-
tory. And eye contact was minimal.

In those days, Shakey's often had someone sitting at
the piano, energetically playing honky-tonk music. I
think it was supposed to fit in with the nineties' motif
and, more generally, lift one's spirits. It doesn't work.
Not on me, at least. I like honky-tonk about as much as
lying on the beach. Added to my mood and the stimulating conversation, then, was a young woman, banging
away on the keyboard, testing the limits of the piano, not
to mention my eardrums.

While I was looking at the menu, I noticed Heather
whispering something to Judy. Her mother nodded and,
in short order, Heather was scooting out of her seat,
running down the aisle, and heading over to the piano
player.

"What's she planning to do?" I asked curiously.

"She wants to ask the pianist to play something,"
Judy responded.

"I didn't know this was a request program," I said
sarcastically. "What is she going to ask her to play?" Judy
shrugged her shoulders.

I watched as Heather walked up to the pianist and
waited patiently for her to finish her "song." Eventually,
the thing ended, and Heather managed to make her
request. The pianist didn't seem to mind and soon
Heather was back in her chair, her head just poking over
the top of the table.

"Well . . . ," I said finally, "what did you ask her to
play?"

"Jesus Loves Me," she replied in a ho-hum manner.

"What!" I barked incredulously.

"Jesus Loves Me," she shouted with equal gusto,
assuming I couldn't hear.

I looked at Judy in disbelief. With something

resembling a smirk, she shrugged her shoulders and said, "It's her favorite song."

I was still trying to figure out my own feelings on the subject when the pianist went into her next tune. I didn't recognize it at first—it was an introduction of some sort—but it definitely was not honky-tonk. And it was beautiful.

Before long it became obvious what she was playing. It was "Jesus Loves Me." Not just any old rendition of "Jesus Loves Me," I might add, but a highly nuanced version that changed keys periodically and used the entire keyboard. When she finished playing it once, she played it a second time, this time using a different style. This happened again after her second go-around, and again after her third. In all, she played six different versions of "Jesus Loves Me" that evening, each one more beautiful than the next. I sat there transfixed.

When the performance came to a conclusion, Heather jumped off her seat and scooted down the aisle for a second time.

"What's she up to this time?" I asked, more like a chastened child than an inquisitive father.

"She wants to thank her for playing 'Jesus Loves Me,'" Judy responded.

Again I watched as Heather carried on a conversation with the pianist. This time they talked for quite a while, after which the young woman took Heather in her arms and gave her a big hug.

"What happened, Heather?" I asked as she made her way back to our table.

"Oh . . . ," she replied casually, as she bit into her pizza, "she just asked me if I loved Jesus. I said, 'Yes,' and then she told me, 'I love Jesus, too.' And then she gave me a big hug. That's all. She's a very nice lady, you know, Daddy. She's my friend."

"I know, honey," I said. "I know."

We find friends in the most unusual places. Or our children find them for us. They do that—our children—because they have not yet discovered the utility of ignoring people or using them as checkers, bus drivers, or honky-tonk pianists. Children are naïve. They haven't learned the rules for living in the modern world. They see no reason to ignore the fact that people are more than the roles they play. And so they can't see any reason why a honky-tonk pianist wouldn't want to play "Jesus Loves Me."

And who, knowing the love of Jesus, would think otherwise? Only adults, who are rooted more firmly in modern life than in the love of Christ. And, therefore, live among strangers. And angels, unaware.

Friends

I seem to acquire my friends by default—by the fault of someone else, that is. I don't know why, but for some reason I typically assume I'm not going to like people before I meet them. I'll see some new chap in church, and instead of running over and shaking his hand and introducing him to others, my natural inclination is to say, "Nah, not my type. I'll let someone else make the intros this morning." That's obviously not the most effective approach to evangelism, nor has it endeared me to members of the hospitality committee. But, as I say, it's what comes naturally.

I realize this may sound odd after what I said in the last chapter about strangers, the beach, and the modern world. One might assume that, in reaction to the anonymity of modern life, I would go out of my way to be friendly to strangers. But that's not the case and small-town people will know why. My complaint about the modern world, remember, is that we are *careless* about one another, not that people don't like each other. People who live in small towns don't necessarily like their neighbors, for instance, but they know them and they treat them—for good or ill—as if they are people. We Moderns, on the other hand, find it easy to like people, but easier still to use them or ignore them all together. In my case, I wish I didn't live among so many strangers. But I do. And unfortunately, I don't particularly like them.

What this means, of course, is that there are an awful lot of wonderful people out there who I never get to know. And more to the point, those that do become my friends, do so almost inadvertently. Or even against my will. Or because of the intervention of other people, like my wife, who automatically assumes the best about everyone.

Such was the case with Steve. Steve is a fellow I met in college. Actually, I didn't really meet him, I just knew of him. I graduated from a fairly small college so one had some information about almost everyone on campus, whether one really knew them or not. But Steve was an outstanding athlete and that meant it was hard not to know of him. In fact, by the time he graduated from college, he was well on his way to becoming a world-class decathlete. Though he and I traveled in different circles, I was more than aware of his existence.

And of course, I didn't like him. Simply the fact that I didn't know him well was adequate grounds for disliking him. But I had other reasons too. You see, my greatest achievement in track-and-field occurred in fifth grade, when I managed to come in second place in a high-jump contest. Second place is not bad, you're thinking, and high jump is a fairly prestigious event. That is true. The problem, however, is that there were only three of us in the contest. It turns out all the good athletes were running the 100-yard dash at the time. I later learned that any of the top ten sprinters could have outperformed me, which they did with great gusto in all track meets from that time hence.

You should also know that as a child I had great aspirations about athletics in general, not only in high jump, but also in football, baseball, and especially basketball. Growing up, I spent hours shooting baskets and pitching baseballs, practicing for what was sure to be a memorable career. Actually, I didn't so much practice for my career as pretend I already had one. Every shot came at the buzzer with the crowd going crazy; every pitch came in the World Series at the completion of a perfect game. If I was to make my mark anywhere, I thought it was going to be in athletics.

This dream required the cooperation of others, however, and that proved to be a bit of a problem. People, and especially coaches, kept intruding in my plans. There was the baseball coach in seventh grade, for example, who didn't think I was good enough to play first-string catcher merely because my throw to second base bounced a few times before reaching the second baseman.

And then there was the freshman basketball coach who cut me from the team simply because I was four-foot-ten and hadn't yet acquired a jump shot. Actually, I had the shot down pretty well, but the jumping part was a problem. I put a lot of energy into it but my feet rarely went more than two inches off the ground. I told the coach that it was a congenital defect, but I didn't receive much sympathy. He was blindly committed to the idea that a four-foot-ten basketball player needed more than a two-inch jump shot.

Finally, there was a second freshman basketball coach who also cut me from the squad, even though I was now a sophomore and had grown a good six inches. This was the ultimate blow because it meant my future career as a Celtic was in jeopardy. Since juniors weren't allowed to play on the freshman team, I couldn't give it another try the year after. And even in my dreams I could not imagine that I would be able to replace Bob Cousey without at least a modicum of high-school experience. I had to admit, as well, that the two-inch jump shot would be a problem in the pros. I walked home that night, knowing that my athletic career was over and singing, "You'll Never Walk Alone."

I did bounce back from that tragedy by becoming a fairly decent tennis player. I lettered a few times, our team won the league championship, and I even managed to compete in regional tournaments. Tennis had a few other advantages as well, I discovered, the most significant being that it put me in the fast lane periodically, opening to me the world of racquet clubs, saunas, and parking lots full of Mercedes and Porsches. And I could live with that. But tennis was not capable of putting my athletic career back on track or rescuing the dreams of my youth. And I never could get rid of the sneaking suspicion that I only made the tennis team because all the good athletes were playing baseball and running track.

By the time I arrived at college, I had replaced athletic aspirations with other things. To an outside observer, there were no visible wounds to my ego and, on the whole, I thought I had forgotten about my disappointment with sports. Deep down, however, I must have harbored a degree of bitterness because whenever I met someone who had really made it in sports I automatically disliked them. Especially if I didn't know them.

Given all of this, Steve didn't stand a chance. As a stranger and a superstar, he already had two strikes against him. But he also struck me as a "jock," who hung around with other jocks, without much interest in the finer things of life. Like language. Indeed, in the few times I had met him he managed to communicate almost exclusively through frowns, grunts, and other primordial gestures. I had no doubt that these came in handy on the athletic field and in the locker room, but they hardly seemed the basis of a friendship.

To this litany of discontent, I must add one more thing. Steve had a girlfriend. And she was beautiful. I don't think I'm revealing any great secret by saying that guys loathe other guys with beautiful girlfriends. This is pure jealousy, of course, and it fits right in with the naturally competitive instincts of most American males. But when you add it to the fact that Steve was a stranger, a superstar, a jock, and seemingly a linguistic caveman— well, you will see that I had many reasons to despise him, which I did, and little reason to be his friend, which I wasn't.

But then a funny thing happened. His girlfriend, Emily, and mine—the infamous Judy Brinkman, re- nowned fly stitcher and soon to become mother of our children—were both chosen to be on the homecoming court. This meant that they were involved in a number of exciting events together (like staying up all night build- ing a float after which they were required to sit on it for four hours, showing teeth and waving hands). Well all of these fun times spawned an immediate bond between them, and Emily and Judy became fast friends. (The speed at which they developed their friendship always bothered me, I might add. Why was there no rivalry between them anyway? I was jealous of Steve for having such a beautiful girlfriend; why wasn't Emily jealous of Judy for having a hunk like me for a boyfriend? I'm perplexed to this day.)

What all of this comes down to is that, in due time, Joe Decathlon and I found ourselves in one another's company, not because either of us wanted to be but because we were dating women who wanted to be. Needless to say, this led to some awkward moments. I remember sitting with Emily and Steve at the homecom- ing banquet and not saying a thing until we were halfway through the meal. Both Steve and I acted as if such silence was the manly thing to do, and I even pretended to be interested in the nonstop conversation between Emily and Judy. Eventually, I thought it was important to let Steve know that I could talk—whether he could or not was still an open question—and so I decided to ask him about something within his own area of expertise.

"So, Steve," I said as I crossed my arms in front of me, "how's your baton?" Steve looked perplexed and I wasn't sure he was even going to answer me. He finally just scrunched up his face and quizzically asked.

"My what?"

"Your baton, Steve, your baton. You know that primitive stick that you guys are always handing off and using to pat one another on the butt with? How's your baton?"

Steve looked at me as if he didn't know whether to spit or cry. "Uh . . . we don't use batons in decathlon," he finally said very slowly, as if he were talking to a retard. "It's a solo sport. Batons are used in relays. Besides, the college owns all the batons. We don't."

I knew all of that, of course, and had thought my question was humorous. It was not, obviously, and now I felt like the person he assumed I was.

I contemplated my next move. In my first foray I had managed to learn not only that Steve could talk, but that I could look pretty stupid in the process. Silence was preferable to this, I concluded. We sat there for a few more minutes, eating and listening to Emily and Judy. Finally, Steve took the initiative.

"Well, Stan, how do you like socialism?"

I was stunned. He wanted to talk about socialism? But why? Socialism is a concept, not a sport (in later days, I would learn that this isn't entirely true, but that's another story). Did Steve really want to talk about ideas?

And why socialism? Why would he associate me with socialism? Suddenly, the lights came on.

"Sociology! You mean my major, sociology! Oh, it's going fine. But you know that socialism is quite different from sociology. One's a political ideology and the other's a discipline. In fact, most sociologists are not . . . ," and as I rambled on, I slowly began to recognize the look on Steve's face. It was my look, just two minutes before, when I had popped a funny, only to have it taken seriously by Steve.

I stopped talking. And in moments, Steve and I were once again fully absorbed in Emily and Judy's conversation. An involvement, I might add, which persisted throughout the evening.

What happened after that is a complicated story. But suffice it to say, Steve and I continued to interact because I liked his girlfriend, he liked mine, and our girlfriends liked each other. But not for long. Three things changed rapidly. Within a few months, Emily became Steve's wife, Judy became my wife, and Steve became—would you believe?—one of my best friends.

How did it happen? Well, to be honest with you, I'm not quite sure. I do know that I began to see that many of my preconceptions were wrong. Steve was committed to his sport, that's for sure. But his commitment was neither brainless nor all consuming. In fact, he rarely talked about athletics and almost never about himself. And when the decathlon did come up in a discussion, his comments were always reflective, never self-congratulatory, and unusually dispassionate. As if he had a certain distance from it. I'm sure this had something to do with me (you don't talk sports with someone who thinks a baton is a symbol of camaraderie—I never could convince Steve I was joking), and I suspect the topic of athletics came up a lot more often with his other friends. But in spite of the fact that the decathlon took enormous amounts of energy and discipline, it was not Steve's life. He had other interests.

Over time, I also began to see that there was a lot of depth to the man. That his values were deeply held and that he was not easily swayed from them, regardless of who was doing the swaying. In the late sixties, that was unusual, as it is today. I also discovered that Steve had an unexpectedly bizarre sense of humor; but propriety and friendship keeps me from providing any details on that score. Suffice it to say, his humor gave balance to a time of intense studies, burning cities, and peers marching off to war. In other words, Steve was part of the survival package that God put together for me at that time in my life.

But maybe the most important thing is that Steve was interested in me. He asked me questions and took time to listen. I started out thinking that he wasn't a talker. I ended up discovering that he talked when he had something to say. But, just as importantly, he listened. That's rare in my experience. Many people want to be your friend so they can tell you about themselves. And that's fine, I suppose, because we all need people to talk to. But they will not become a friend until they start asking questions. And take the time to listen.

That's especially true for me because I'm not a natural talker. My students will no doubt find that humorous, but it's true nevertheless. I grew up in an extended family where there was a great deal of verbal repartee and debate. But it was thought impolite to dominate a conversation. And no one carried on a monologue. As a result, I learned to ask questions, give brief answers, and keep the banter going. When I get in a situation where no one asks me questions, however, I'm stuck. I just listen, throw in a question every now and then, and listen some more. I simply can't bear the thought of saying something no one really wants to hear.*

But Steve listened. And talked. And soon, I began to enjoy his company. To like him. To like myself when I was with him. To feel safe in his presence—about blundering or not talking or just making a fool out of myself. And so both Steve and Emily became good friends. A safe haven for a couple of restless souls, floundering along at the beginning of a marriage career. And twenty years later, they are. Still.

Friends are like that, I think. In the presence of a friend, there is a comfort and a restfulness like no other. When I was young, we used to sing about Jesus as our friend. Our comforter and our peace. As I grew older, I came to dislike this language because it seemed to ignore the prophetic side of the Gospel, and to make The Christ mundane.

And that can happen. Especially in the modern world—where the self is king and tolerance justifies any conclusion—it is easy for Christ's friendship to be trivialized and the salvation he offers reduced to cheap grace.

But that doesn't obviate the fact that Jesus is a friend—indeed, the grandest friend of all. The problem is, there are so many things that come between us and his friendship. Or more precisely, so many things that prevent us from fully accepting it.

There are people like me, for instance, who resist the unknown, and assume that whoever he is, we won't

*My students may find this statement even harder to believe than the first! But the classroom is defined as a time and place when the prof is supposed to talk; for that reason, talking comes easily for me there. It is my social obligation, after all. Nevertheless, even in class, if I detect that my students don't care about the topic, it bothers me terribly. That is why I jump up and down in class and tell so many stupid stories. I'm just too insecure to carry on a lecture to a bunch of bored students. And their time is too valuable to waste.

like him. We are the ones who are happy in our own little worlds, at home with the familiar. Unwilling to admit we have needs, we cut ourselves off from others.

We are turned off by his superstar status as well, some of us. And by the hype that surrounds him. Besides, we're awfully busy trying to be superstars ourselves. Who needs competition, after all?

Most distressingly, there are those friends of his, the people he runs around with. What a motley crew they are. So imperfect. So crude. So ... not like us. If he's anything like his followers, who would want to have anything to do with him?

But then we find ourselves in the same room with him one day. And after a few faltering starts at conversation, we slowly begin to discover that he's not the man we thought he was. He doesn't talk about himself, for one thing, but rather those he came to serve. And the One who sent him.

His interests are far flung, including, he says, the whole world. And best of all, he listens. And questions. And listens some more. He does not affirm all that we say. And some of his questions are not fun to answer. But no answer is beyond his capacity to listen. And no question will turn him away.

What would you think of a friend like that? One who would not reject you, regardless of how stupid your answers were? Who would not tell you a lie, regardless of how much you wanted to hear it?

And what would you think if this same person said, without embarrassment, that he loved you? Indeed, loved you so much that he would accept guilt for every wrong you ever committed—from the time you threw a cat off the roof to the day you told God to go jump in a lake— and take your punishment for you? And if necessary, would die for you. Has died for you. Because it was necessary. To liberate you from your present hell. And all hells to come.

Probably, you'd think he was the biggest liar to ever walk the face of the earth. Or a godsend. And the kind of friend you've been looking for all your life.

10

LIFE AS
GOD

Receiving

My conversion story is not unlike others that I have heard about over the years. And being raised evangelical, I've heard quite a few. Not that we talked about our conversions all the time. One didn't normally begin dinner with the announcement, "I accepted the Lord while in the middle of a storm. . . ."

Nevertheless, at certain times it inevitably came up. Like during baptismal classes. Or daily vacation Bible school. Or the ubiquitous summer church camp, where adolescents throw faggots on the fire, confess to unspeakable sins, make unkeepable promises, and relate unbelievable testimonies. Trust me. I've heard about many conversions.

And as I say, mine was not unique. Nor especially exciting from the perspective of good narrative. I was about seven years old at the time, immersed in the things that seven-year-olds typically immerse themselves in. Like playing cops and robbers. Going to the second grade. And annoying my older brother and sister. In the midst of all this important activity, my mom suddenly burst into my room one day and asked, "Stanley, do you know the Lord?"

Now, my mom can be blunt sometimes, but she is not normally confrontive. Our relationship, from the beginning, was fairly intuitive, and we found it easy to laugh and talk and argue. There were a few rough years during adolescence, when I exercised my independence and she was not thrilled by the exercise program (she was especially unnerved the day I came home with my head shaven; hair is important to moms, I discovered). But this period in our relationship lasted no more than twenty years. And it was undergirded by a foundation of love. There has never been a moment in my life that I haven't known, absolutely, that Mom loved me. And that's not a bad legacy. If my children can say that about me when they turn forty, I will consider my life a success.

So it was a surprise to me when Mom came in my room with the big question. I mean, the BIG question. I don't know what provoked it. Probably my behavior, but I can't remember being especially difficult that day. Maybe it just came out of the blue, a spontaneous act, provoked by a mother's concern for her son's well-being. On the other hand, maybe she had it written on her calendar: "May 6—Pick up detergent. Call Alvina about PTA program. And ask Stanley if he knows the Lord." Who knows the ways of a mom. Or our Lord.

Anyway, there I was, playing in my room and being my own sweet self, when my mother unloaded El Primo on me. Now, there are many ways one can respond to such a question. There is the right way ("You bet, Mom; Jesus loves me this I know"), after which your mom will pat you on the head, and say, "Aren't you a sweetie pie." There is the wrong way ("Uh . . . Lord who?"), after which she will say, "Go back to your blocks." And then there is my way ("What? Oh . . . well, sure. I mean, I go to church, don't I?'') after which come the dreaded words, "Stanley, we need to talk."

At first, I tried to defend my position. After all, I did go to church. True, I had no choice in the matter. But that seemed a minor detail. The fact is, I had sat through many sermons in my young life, heard a variety of Sunday-school lessons, and knew at least fifty Bible stories backward and forward. Moreover, I knew about Jesus. I knew he walked on water. I knew he had told his disciples to bug off when they tried to prevent children from getting near him ("Yea, Jesus!"). And I knew that he had healed my big toe when it accidentally connected with the cigarette lighter in the car and had to heal real quickly—before my next bath—so my mom wouldn't see the telltale rings of fire. It did. She didn't. And I knew Jesus was responsible.

So, on the whole, it seemed to me that Jesus was on my side. And that was pretty good evidence, I thought, that I knew the Lord. Mom was not convinced, however. "You can know an awful lot about Jesus," she said, "without really having him in your heart. The church is full of people who read the Bible and do all the right things, but don't really love the Lord."

Boy, she had me there. I could think of two or three people in our church who were always there on Sunday morning but had a scowl on their faces that would have made Howdy-Doody wince.

"You mean like Mr. V—" I began, only to be cut short.

"It's no concern of yours who they are, Stanley. Man looks at the outward appearance but God looks at the heart. God knows and that's all that matters. The question is, what does he know about you? Are you one of his children?"

I looked at her and shook my head in a positive manner. But my eyes were full of doubt. And so was my heart. And thus, mothers being heart readers, not head watchers—they're a little like God that way—Mom began telling me (again) the old, old story, a story I had already heard many times before, even though I was only seven. A story of Jesus and his love. And the price that he had paid for me on the cross. Because I needed it. Because God knew I needed it. And because God does not want anyone to remain lost in their neediness forever.

It is a heartbreaking story, if the heart wants to listen. And this time mine did. It may have been a seven-year-old's awareness of evil that made the difference (you've seen a lot of sin by the age of seven; you've already had a couple of years of recess, remember). It may have been the fact that no one wanted to play with me that day. But the thing I remember most clearly, and the thing that continues to choke me up each time I eat the bread and drink the wine, is the amazing love of Christ. On the cross. Undeservedly. For me.

And so I asked Jesus into my heart. Which is a seven-year-old's way of telling God, "I'm sorry," "I need help," and "Thank you," all in one phrase. And my heart took wings. Literally. I remember running from room to room, from inside to out, so excited that I couldn't sit down. I remember hugging my mom with the delight of a returning prodigal son. I even remember doing the unthinkable, which was sharing my Good News with my brother and sister. There was no small risk in that move because older brothers and sisters take great joy in squelching the jubilation of younger siblings. But not this time. For they too had heard the Good News. And besides, I didn't care about risks on that day or the consequences of my pride. The news was just too good to keep to myself, and my pride, too small a matter to care.

I recall another day, some fourteen years later, when my heart again took wings. It was in the middle of my junior year in college and it was preceded (again) by the realization that I was in trouble, that I was a needy human being. That realization hit me while I was sitting in a bathtub, as a matter of fact, and that's probably no great surprise since I suspect most of us feel vulnerable while taking a bath. But you'll need more background than that to get the impact of the moment.

The important thing you need to know is that although I had been dating Judy for only about two months, I was already pretty sure that she was the one. In fact, I was fairly confident of that fact the day I laid eyes on her. Now that comment could be misconstrued, especially since you already know that I'm inclined to make visual judgments. And it sounds like I just fell in love with the first pretty face that came my way. But that's not quite right.

I'll admit, I was drawn to Judy because of her looks. She is beautiful. But you don't have to watch her for long before you can see much more than how she looks. Judy's not at all opaque. Her laugh, her manner, her very presence tells you exactly who she is. So when I say that it was love at first sight, I'm not talking merely of lust. I'm saying that, very quickly, I knew a great deal about her. And I fell head over heels in love with what I knew.

You should also know that I was not exactly inexperienced in the area of female companionship. Certainly, I was no Don Juan and I always felt more than a bit awkward about the whole dating enterprise. Nevertheless, I gave it the old college try. And from about the first grade on, I had a series of romantic interests, most of which lasted a duration of at least two to three hours. Now, there are only two things about these interests that you should—or ever will—know. One, on the whole, they involved marvelous human beings. I kid you not, I was blessed with the nicest girlfriends you ever wanted to see. Quality people. And second, from these dating experiences I became convinced that the "right" person didn't exist. Not for me.

The problem was not that I had a hard time falling for someone. Falling in love was a piece of cake. The problem was that it seemed impossible to get the right heart and soul and mind and body all combined into a person who thought you were the right heart and soul and mind and body. Sometimes the face was right but the mouth wouldn't stop talking. At other times, the mind was beautiful but the body was not. And more than I cared to admit, sometimes the combination was delightful but I was not.

But the major obstacle, I came to believe, was this matter of the soul. And by the time I was in high school, I had convinced myself that my dating problem was primarily the result of being a Christian—as did everyone else in my youth group. We'd all sit around on Sunday night after church, look at each other, and say, "Gee, are you the only thing I've got to pick from?" And I know my presence was a real disappointment to many an aspiring young maiden.

My solution was to try to put all the other elements together and forget about the Christian part. After all, I wasn't planning to get married right away. Indeed, I wasn't planning to get married at all. I just wanted to have a good time. That's what I told myself anyway, and it wasn't the least bit convincing. I understood that my approach was a high-risk maneuver. All the books on teen dating said so and we know what a powerful influence they have. Besides, each time I started to get the least bit serious about someone, I realized that I was looking at a potential marriage partner. And it was scary. Because I wasn't sure I had the resolve to tear myself away from a relationship for that reason alone.

In hindsight, it is clear that I was protected from my own stupidity during this time. Most relationships didn't work out. And the ones that did were always terminated for other reasons. But in the end, I was left with the very strong conviction that putting me together with the right person was going to be a nearly impossible task. If I tingled, they did not. And if they tingled, I did not. "In Search of the Mutual Tingle" was the story of my life. And I feared the story would not have a happy ending.

One last thing. Added to all this gloom-and-doom was the lurking suspicion that I didn't deserve to find the mutual tingle. I can't go into or fully explain this suspicion. I surmise it resulted from a very superficial view of God, as someone who punished past sins by making life difficult in the future. But I had not been an Eagle Scout. Though I would guess my behavior was about average for a churchgoing adolescent (not exactly the Betty Crocker Seal of Approval), my heart was a cesspool of mixed motivations. And it seemed altogether reasonable to me that a Holy God would exact a high price for such unholiness. In other words, I didn't really believe that my redemption at the age of seven had covered the whole bill.

Given all of this, you can now see what an absolute joy it was to find Judy. It was, for the first time in my life, the coming together of all the elements. Mind, soul, body—you name it, she had it. And I knew that she had it from the beginning. What I couldn't be sure of was whether I had it. Would I be the right combination for her? That, from day one, was the only question as far as I was concerned. That's how sure I was about Judy.

About two months into our relationship, however, something unforeseen happened. We had been dating steadily and everything seemed to be proceeding along nicely. Fabulously, in fact. I became more and more convinced that Judy was a very special human being.

And she, in turn, seemed to like me. I was beginning to think that, maybe, just maybe, the impossible had finally happened.

And then, from out of nowhere, came this incredible curveball. As Judy and I were walking back to her dorm one evening, she suddenly told me she was thinking of transferring to another school next year. At first, I thought she was just thinking out loud, throwing out a number of random ideas about the future. But the more we talked, the more it became clear that she was seriously considering transferring to a college back east. She said she thought the change would do her good. That she would enjoy studying in a different environment.

Well, I was devastated—which means that I stopped talking and began thinking. How could this be, I asked myself? If she's as serious about me as I am about her, how could she possibly consider transferring? And for no particular reason! I mean, if she needed to transfer for academic reasons or to get another major—that would be understandable. But to transfer simply to experience a new environment? Why would she do that? Why would she be thinking of leaving me in order to study amongst a different set of trees? It didn't compute.

Unless—and I reached this "unless" the next morning while I was sitting in the bathtub—unless I wasn't nearly as important to her as I had assumed. Unless I was just one more in a long string of male companions who would come into her life for a time and then depart for parts unknown. Unless all my assumptions about the fit between mind and soul and heart and body were wrong. Unless God was finally exacting the revenge I had been expecting all along, letting me walk way out to the very end of the limb before snapping it off. Unless she didn't really love me.

"Lord, please don't let this happen," I cried, as I slowly extricated myself from the bath and began dressing for the day. "After all the searching. After all the false starts and disappointing relationships. After all the pain. To finally get this close and then have the whole thing slip into the abyss. I just don't think my heart could bear it. Please, Lord, don't let this happen."

I concluded that the possibilities were just too devastating to live with. I had to know what Judy was thinking. I picked up the phone and dialed her number. No one answered. She was probably in class. I went to breakfast in a stupor. Ate my muffin in silence. Walked over to the library in an attempt to hit the books. Stared at page 253 for about one hour. Went back to my room. Picked up the phone again and dialed Judy's number.

"Good morning, Suite E," came an anonymous voice on the other end of the line.

"Hi, sweety," I responded without the slightest attempt at humor. "Is Judy there?"

"I think so, Stan. Just a sec."

The seconds turned into minutes, and the minutes, hours, before I heard her voice on the other end of the line. "Hello?"

"Hi Judy, this is Stan."

"Good morning, Stan. What's—"

"Judy, I need to talk with you. Now. Can I came over in a few minutes?"

"Well ...," she hesitated, "I'm studying for an exam that's coming up this afternoon. And I told my roommate that I'd stick around and catch the phone in case her mom called. I really shouldn't—"

"It's kind of important," I broke in. "How 'bout if I come to your back window. We can talk through the screen. It won't take long."

"Well ...," She said. "Okay. If it's important."

I hung up and began the half-mile journey to her dormitory. The conversation on the phone had not gone well. She sounded distant. Uneasy. I knew that I'd been brisk but she was usually able to turn the other cheek, rarely returning my poor manners in kind. This time, however, she had responded like everyone else in the world. Forcefully. And by the time I had reached her back window, I had the feeling that I was about to have my worst suspicions realized.

"Judy. Are you there?" I called.

She came to the full-length window and cranked open the pane. She was wearing a long-sleeved flannel nightgown but I could tell that she had been up for a while. I started out with an apology.

"I'm sorry to bother you now, Judy. I know this wasn't very convenient."

"Oh, it's okay," she said with a smile. "I'm just worried about this exam. And I didn't want to take the time right now to get dressed and prepare myself to meet the world. What's on your mind?"

"Judy," I began haltingly, "Judy, I've been thinking about our talk last night. You know, when you said that you were thinking about transferring to another college next year?"

She shook her head in agreement.

"Well," I continued, "what does that mean? About us, anyway? I mean, I don't want to leave this campus. Not next year, next week, or next second. Not if you're here. I want to be where you are. With you. And, well, I just don't see how you can be thinking about leaving either. . . ."

It was a bold declaration at that point in our relationship. For though we'd been dating for two months already, we had only expressed our affection in acts and gestures, not in words. Most of all, we had not made any commitments to each other. It was a relationship built on deeds, not promises, and the future had been left without definition.

Judy looked at me for a moment without saying

anything. And then, maintaining her silence, she cranked open the screen, climbed through the window, wrapped her arms around me and laid her head against my chest.

"Stan, you big dummy. Don't you know that I love you? And that I wouldn't want to go anywhere without you?"

I really don't remember what happened after that. How she explained her comments about transferring. What I said in response to her declaration of love. How long we stood there hugging each other before she finally slipped back through the window and resumed studying for her afternoon exam. I only remember walking back to my car, slipping into the driver's seat, and realizing that this was finally it. That she really loved me. And that a dream of a lifetime had come true.

And my heart again took wings. Discovering myself behind the wheel of a car, I started to drive. And for the next hour or so, I found myself wandering around the back roads of Santa Barbara. Up the hills. Down along the beach. Onto the freeway and off onto a little dirt road. And everywhere I went, I told the world what I had learned. Every passing car heard the good news. Every tree and hill was informed of my good fortune. For all of creation just had to know. She loved me. Judy Lynn Brinkman loved me.

Giving

Two flights of the heart. Both set off by confessions of need and love. And both resulting in joy. And wonder. And the uncontrollable urge to share the moment with others. True, there is a great difference between the two. For one involved a relationship between God and man, and the other, between a man and a woman. And that difference is nothing short of profound.

But it was the apparent chasm between these two events that led to my surprise when I discovered their similarities in the first place. The time that Judy expressed her love for me seemed like a discreet event in my life. Unlike anything I had ever experienced before. The same was true when I first declared my faith in Christ. That too stood alone. As something without parallel or equal.

These two events were further kept apart in my mind by the two very different roles that I played in each one. In the case of my conversion, I was the one whose love was sought. God declared his love for me, long before I ever reciprocated. "For God so loved the world that he . . ." His love came first. The Hound of Heaven pursued me, not the reverse. And at the age of seven, through the kind auspices of my mother, I finally managed to reciprocate.

In the case of Judy, however, the situation was clearly reversed. For it was I who was in pursuit. Not that Judy had to beat me off with a stick or anything like that. And not that she even wanted to. But it was I who was the hound of the hallowed halls of ivy, not Judy. And it was I who eventually sought to make her my wife.

Nevertheless, the consequences for me were identical. Whether it was love given or love finally received, it didn't matter a whit. It was still a moment of reconciliation. A season of great joy. And a time to share the good news with others.

And that started me thinking. About God. And about his feelings concerning this matter of reconciliation. For some reason, that thought had never crossed my mind before. Certainly, I assumed that the Lord was pleased when one of his children came home. But I didn't assume he got too worked up over the matter, either. After all, he was God. The All-Knowing, All-Seeing, Creator of heaven and earth. These things happened to him everyday. Surely, he had better things to do than rejoice in the love declarations of his children.

But that's not how I felt when Judy declared her love for me. I was ecstatic. Granted, I'm not God. And part of my joy came simply from the fact that I was surprised by its presence. To that extent, it was a joy born of ignorance. But what God lacks in ignorance must be more than made up for by his knowledge. His knowledge of what we have been redeemed from. His knowledge of the real cost of our redemption. His knowledge of the future it has afforded us. All of these can only make our declaration of faith and love more meaningful in his eyes. More significant. More joyful.

And so I have begun to wonder. Could it be that our

expressions of love—in word and deed—bring unbridled joy to the very heart of God? Could it be that his heart takes wings at the return of even one of his many prodigals? Could it be that the news is so good that all of heaven hears about it, and all of creation too? Could it be that love's ecstasy is not confined to me? Or you?

That thought came home to me again this Christmas, some twenty years after Judy confessed her love for me while standing in a nightgown, and not quite forty years since the day I confessed my love for Christ at my mother's side.

By way of preface, you should know that at our house Christmas is not the simple event it was the night Mary gave birth to Jesus. We insist on improving things. And so we have developed this elaborate ritual to celebrate the birth of Christ. It begins on December first with Advent readings and surprises of various kinds. And it culminates on Christmas Day with a complicated series of munchings, worship, and gift giving. I don't know how we came up with the formula but each year something new seems to get added to the ritual. And, because Heather has a memory like an elephant, nothing is ever eliminated.

What this means, of course, is that when we finally get to the gift-giving phase of the ritual, the kids are about ready to explode. Especially our youngest, Kirsten. She has had it with the appetizers. She wants the main course. Like Christian parents everywhere, we have explained to her that the gifts are not the main course— that something much more important is going on—and, like children everywhere, she just assumes that's one more in a long series of stupid things that parents seem compelled to say. If there is anything more fun than opening presents, she hasn't found it yet. Which, at the age of five, is essentially true.

Anyway, it was while we were in the midst of the

gift-giving portion of our ceremony—as I was watching Kirsten rip into one of her presents—that I was suddenly overcome with déjà vu. And I remembered myself in Kirsten's place as a young child, similarly opening my own gifts with great gusto and glee. But I didn't only recall opening up presents. I also remembered looking up at my mom and dad, and seeing them sitting on the couch with their assortment of cheap perfumes, socks, and all the other ridiculous gifts that children perpetually purchase for their parents.

Wow, I recalled thinking to myself, *am I glad I'm not a parent. They get the dumbest gifts in the world!*

But I also remembered watching their faces, my mom's and dad's. And do you know what I saw? They didn't look like people who were receiving dumb gifts at all. Indeed, Mom and Dad weren't paying any attention to their own presents whatsoever. They were watching us, instead. And smiling. And having the time of their lives.

And now here I was, almost forty years later, sitting on my own couch, holding my own allotment of cheap perfumes and socks and underwear. And watching my own children. And smiling. And knowing, at last, why my parents enjoyed Christmas despite the quality of their gifts.

But, you know, I also couldn't help but think how warped my vision had been as a little boy. How self-centered. How totally immersed in its own world. All I could think about then was the joy of receiving a little Christmas booty. And the fact that my parents were having the time of their lives—giving me those presents—just passed me right by.

Sometimes I think we're a little like that when it comes to the matter of God's relationship with us. Like children everywhere, we enjoy the gifts he gives us. And when we finally open our eyes enough to see his greatest gift of all, the Gift of Christ, we're so overjoyed by the occasion itself that we scarcely notice the joy of the Giver.

It may be that, like parents everywhere, God doesn't mind our forgetfulness. That it is enough for him to have us willingly receive his precious Gift and to find the joy therein.

But it isn't enough for me. And it shouldn't be enough for anyone else who has received the Gift of Christ either. For if we can't imagine the joy that our love brings to God, then how can we say that we really understand his love for us? And if we remain ignorant of God's love for us, then haven't we cheated ourselves from knowing the greatest wonder the world has ever beheld?

And that's one of the problems with the fast lane. It is full of ambitious people moving at breakneck speeds, which makes it easy to become so focused on the traffic ahead that you let life pass you right by. So anxious to get to the gift, you ignore the giver. So eager to get to the delivery room, you nearly miss the delivery. So anxious to get to church, you forget to execute its mission. So depressed by a day of anonymity at the beach, you ignore those who are trying to befriend you. So consumed by your own inabilities, you can't appreciate the abilities of others. So worried about your future, you can't even enjoy a good bath—or the God who holds the future in his hands.

But then one day—against your will—you suddenly find yourself stuck in the slow lane. And the most peculiar things begin to happen. An act of creation takes place right before your eyes. A five-year-old child offers conclusive evidence that you are not God. A creepy creature becomes an old woman in need. A honky-tonk pianist reminds you of Jesus' love. A presumed enemy becomes a true friend. The object of your affection says, "I love you."

And all at once, a whole new world unfolds before your eyes. Like opening up a gift at Christmas and discovering that the Lord of all creation finds joy in loving you.